W9-BEK-801

Stir
What
You've
Got!

RAYMOND E. BALCOMB

ABINGDON PRESS NASHVILLE AND NEW YORK

Stir What You've Got!

And
Other
Stewardship
Studies

STIR WHAT YOU'VE GOT!

Copyright © 1968 by Abingdon Press

All rights in this book are reserved.
No part of the book may be reproduced in any
manner whatsoever without written permission of
the publishers except brief quotations embodied in
critical articles or reviews. For information address
Abingdon Press, Nashville, Tennessee.

ISBN 0-687-39490-2

Library of Congress Catalog Card Number: 68-17443

Scripture quotations unless otherwise noted are from the Revised
Standard Version of the Bible, copyrighted 1946 and 1952 by the
Division of Christian Education, National Council of Churches, and
are used by permission.

The poem "The Master's Man" by William George Tarrant from
Masterpieces of Religious Verse, edited by James D. Morrison, is re-
printed by permission of Harper & Row, Publishers.

SET UP, PRINTED, AND BOUND BY THE
PARTHENON   PRESS,   AT   NASHVILLE,
TENNESSEE, UNITED STATES OF AMERICA

This is for
Hazel

FOREWORD

"A well-ordered mind in a time of crisis," Robert Louis Stevenson once observed, "is like a clock in a thunderstorm. It just keeps up its regular ticking." This is a book for the Christian layman who is baffled and buffeted by the winds of renewal, dialogue, secularity, existentialism, the death of God controversy, and a score of other theological fads in contemporary American religious life. I do not mean lightly or scornfully to dismiss contemporary theological discussion. It is fun for the pros and will surely yield a worthy distillate, but it helps the layman very little.

I think that a religious recession is under way and that it may well last a good part of a generation (just as the post–World War II religious boom did). And I believe that the faith will survive, as it always has, among relatively small groups of people who take it seriously enough to give it complete commitment.

Hence this book on stewardship. No doctrine of Christianity is more basic or helpful than the contention that God is the creator and owner of all things and that man is meant to be a steward, a trustee, a caretaker. It is found in the story of Adam and Eve, and it applies to tomorrow's church-community action project. It is the nub of a good deal of what the serious artists, writers, and moviemakers—both secular and religious—are saying: "Our age . . . if it believes in salvation of any sort, believes that it comes through the assumption of unlimited liability." [1]

Whatever form or forms a renewed Christianity may take, it (or they) will in some way recover the seriousness of discipline. The average church, for example, does not have as much discipline with respect to attendance as a Rotary club does. It does not have as much discipline with respect to paying the institution's bills as a country club does. It does not have as much discipline with respect to confronting the opposition as a labor union does. It does not have as much discipline over the moral decisions and actions of its members as a medical or bar association does. We have very nearly lost any sense of the church as a community of the faithful which makes demands upon us and exercises authority over us. A good place to begin, it seems to me, is with the recovery of disciplined giving, tithing or more, before taxes. I hope this little book contributes to that end.

RAYMOND E. BALCOMB

[1] Kenneth Rexroth, "The Pilgrim's Progress," *Saturday Review*, August 13, 1966, p. 20.

CONTENTS

Stir What You've Got!

Is there anyone who could not use more than he has? All of us could use more money than we have. We know what the cartoonist was talking about who showed a husband figuring up the family bills, then remarking to his wife: "We seem to be in the middle-income, upper-outgo group." And we can sympathize with the young man who was discovering the "expensive power of a new affection" and was finally driven to sending the young lady a white orchid with this note attached:

> Let the whiteness of this flower attest the purity of my love for you. Let the price of it measure in millions the joy you bring to me. And let the cellophane on the box represent the window of the poorhouse— where I'll be if this keeps up!

I guess all of us could use more money than we have.

Then again, I suspect that most of us feel as though we could use more talent than we have. When Jascha Heifetz was making his debut as a concert violinist, Mischa Elman, already famous in that field, was sitting with pianist Leopold Godowsky. During the mounting ovations for the boy prodigy Elman remarked to Godowsky, "Isn't it hot in here!" The pianist, who was known for his wit, answered, "Not for pianists." If even the great can feel threatened by their own inadequacy, what about the rest of us? We know that if we had more talent we could do better at our daily work, get ahead faster, earn a bigger income, do more for the community. No one of us, of course, has been left without at least one talent, and some have two and a few five. But every one of us feels that he could use more than he has.

Or, is there anyone who couldn't use more time? The young daughter of a friend of mine came home not long ago and announced that she had been elected "chairman of the world"! It turned out that she was head of a committee making a geography report to the class. But most of us feel at times as though we were almost "chairmen of the world"—so much to do and so little time in which to do it. Who wouldn't spend more time with his family or keep the house looking better or help out more in worthwhile community activities if he only had more time?

The hard reality, however, is that we have about as much as we're ever going to have. Every one of us has all the time there is—twenty-four hours a day. None of us are ever going to get more talent than we have—the best we can do is to sharpen what we have a little by training and experience. Some few of us may eventually get a little more money, but not much. Most of us live our lives in just about the same economic stratum into which we were born or which we reached relatively early in life.

The answer to our predicament was given by a waitress in a Washington, D.C., restaurant during World War II when sugar was one of the rationed commodities. A customer who had already received his share called loudly for more sugar in his coffee. Her answer was a classic in brevity, wisdom, and basic English: "Stir what you've got!" These words are reminiscent of the old rendering of Paul's advice to his younger fellow worker Timothy, "Stir up the gift of God, which is in thee" (II Tim. 1:6 KJV). Let's see where this idea leads us.

I

We can begin by noting that our only hope of getting more done is to *stir what time we've got*. It is true that we often feel like an Egyptian mummy—pressed for time—but it is also true that we have telephones and jets which cut distances from miles to minutes; we have pressure cookers, electric mixers, vacuum cleaners, dishwashers, and dryers which make housekeeping possible in a fraction of the time it used to take; we have methods of production which make it possible for us to produce more in a forty-hour week than our fathers did in sixty or seventy hours. It is probable that we actually have more time of our own than any other generation that ever lived.

A couple of years ago the newspapers had a front-page story about a man whose son in his freshman year at the University of Oregon had complained that he "just did not have enough time to study." During his winter vacation father and son sat down together to figure out where the time was going. "Taking a seven-day week of 168 hours, we discovered that after we had given him eight hours of sleep, three hours a day for meals, time for church on Sunday, class time, and dates on Friday and Saturday nights, he still had sixty-five hours of time for which he could not account." They arranged for the boy to fill out a little form each night, jotting down how each hour had been spent from 7 A.M. to 11 P.M. The result was that the boy's grades rose spectacularly, and he went on to graduate with a fine record!

I suspect that the rest of us—if a scientific study were to be made of the way we use our time, if we had to fill out a precise hour-by-hour report for every day— would not be so very different from that young college student. There would be a lot of hours we couldn't account for. We may feel "busier than an octopus going through a revolving door"—as Fred Allen once put it— but we could do more if we used our time better. Do you need more time? Stir what you've got!

II

In the second place, our best hope of being more accomplished than we are is to *stir what talent we have.* I know a man who has had a very distinguished career. He has held leading posts in the federal government under two different administrations; he has held high posts in the educational world; he makes about three hundred speeches a year. There is no doubt that he is a very busy man, yet he also finds time to be active in his church—not merely representing it on high-level state and national committees, but also serving on its local building committee and teaching a Sunday school class! Now, strangest of all, I do not know anyone who thinks that this man is talented much above the average. He is not a brilliant politician; he is not a great educator or scholar; his speeches are pretty ordinary; his presence is warm but undistinguished. But he has made an amazingly full use of what talents he has.

Julia Wolfe once told of a friendly neighbor of hers who occasionally brought over products of her culinary skill. One day she brought Miss Wolfe a plate of hash which was so delicious that the latter couldn't help remarking about it and asking how she made it. The other's face glowed with pleasure. "Beef is nothing," she said. "Pepper's nothing, onions are nothing; but when I throw myself into the hash—that's what makes it what it is." So it is! Try throwing yourself into your home, your work, your church, your community— that's what makes them what they are. Do you need more talent? Stir what you've got!

III

In the third place, note that *our best hope of having enough money to go around is to stir what we've got.* We never get enough money; almost enough, perhaps, but never enough to do everything we'd like. As a preacher and a lecturer Henry Ward Beecher made considerably more than the President of the United

States. He was once speaking to a ministerial group about his own career, and he said that he had known what it was to have too little. (He had gone to the Plymouth Congregational Church in Brooklyn when it had only forty-seven members, so no one could doubt that it had been something of a struggling situation.) Then he said, "And I have known what it is to have almost enough." So with most of us. Our only real chance lies in making a studied, conscientious, intelligent use of our money.

It is not, of course, as though we were destitute. Most of us are not "up against it" financially. A few of us, to be sure, are living on fixed incomes, and a few of us are between jobs. But most of us, if we represent a cross section of our community, have a family income of around $6,300 a year or more. No one, to be sure, will get rich on such an income; but everyone, if he will, can probably do more with what he's getting.

The importance of what we are saying is revealed in an incident from the life of the famous novelist A. J. Cronin. His first career was medicine, not writing, but something in him had driven him to announce that he was going to write a novel. So he and his family took a summer's vacation on a remote Scottish farm. There—while his wife and two children roamed the woods, gathered shells on the beach, helped the herdsman milk the cows and the dairymaid churn the butter—he chained himself, not without self-pity, to a writing desk in a bleak upstairs room. There were some redeeming moments when his characters seemed to come alive, but

there were also those days when it all seemed like useless drudgery. The worst moment came when he was
about halfway through; he was sick of it all; he yielded
to the impulse to give up the whole project. He took the
manuscript to the back door and threw it on the ash
heap. Drawing a certain sullen self-satisfaction from
giving up, he went for a walk. It was a gray, drizzly
Scottish day, tailored to his mood. Before long he came
upon a farmer patiently and laboriously digging in a
bogged and peaty field. The old man knew that Cronin
had come to the area to write, and he had the ancient
Scotch Presbyterian respect for learning and for men
of letters. Cronin told him what he had done. The
farmer was silent for a long while, silent with disap-
pointment and almost contempt. Then he spoke up.

"No doubt you're the one that's right, Doctor, and I'm the
one that's wrong. . . ." He seemed to look right through
me. "My father ditched this bog all his days and never made
a pasture. I've dug it all my days and I've never made a
pasture. But, pasture or no pasture"—he placed his foot
on the spade—"I cannot help but dig. For my father
knew and I know that if you only dig enough, a pasture
can be made here."

The discouraged author got the idea. He tramped back
to the house, "drenched, shamed, furious," and picked
up the soggy sheets from the ash heap. He dried them in
the kitchen oven and went to work harder than ever

until, for better or for worse, the thing was done. That was his first novel—it has sold over three million copies —*Hatter's Castle*. In its train were to come such books as *The Citadel* and *The Keys of the Kingdom*.

That incident is as suggestive as a parable! Many of us feel that we have "ditched the bog" of our limited means without much success. Yet we know in moments of candor that there are those whose industry and stewardship put us to shame.

Let us not despise our own possibilities! A little more diligent and faithful use of what we have can sometimes make a mighty difference. One night a trainload of refugees from Asian communism pulled into the freight yards of a country where there were American Christian missionaries at work. A tired woman, who carried in one hand all her earthly possessions wrapped up in a handkerchief and in the other a baby, sought the help of a medical missionary. The baby was dying of diphtheria; its face was already taking on a bluish tinge, and it was gasping for breath. The doctor said he was afraid she was too late. She answered that she had come as fast as she could. She had walked a hundred miles to the railway and ridden two hundred more on the freight cars. Her husband was dead. He felt there was only one chance in ten thousand, but he decided to make the effort. In the operating room he inserted a breathing tube into the child's throat and gave it all the antitoxin he had—which was about half as much as would have been used here in the United States—and the youngster began to get better. A couple of days later the mother was pestering the doctor. He thought she was still worrying about the child and said, "Lady, the kiddie is all right. Don't worry. Run along." She asked, "Are you too busy to look at me?" Examination revealed that she had cancer of the breast. The next day he operated on her, and she too recovered. Then he figured out what it had cost to express the love of God in our time: the baby cost $4.67 and its mother cost $16.50—a total of two lives for $21.17. Do you need more money? Stir what you've got!

IV

It is seldom a good idea to exhort people to do something without giving some practical help as to how they can do it. So let us move on to say that *one of the most helpful and practical ways people have ever found to stir what they've got in the way of time and talent and money is to tithe.* Tithing means giving 10 percent or more of what the federal income tax blank calls "total income." It means giving 10 percent or more of your personal or family income for the work of the Lord.

Tithing is not primarily a method of church finance, although churches with tithing members seldom have financial problems. It is primarily a way of living effectively, a way of making a full and complete use of what you have and what you are. If it seems to you that I am overstating it or if you are smiling cynically to yourself that talking about stewardship always "comes down to talking about money," the answer is simple: money

19

to most of us is nothing more or less than a sort of congealed form of human work, ingenuity, creativity, time, and talent applied to the God-given resources of our planet. If I were speaking primarily to farmers who might have more land than money, I might well be speaking about the stewardship of the soil and the conservation of water; if I were speaking primarily to creative artists who might have more time and talent than cash, I might well be speaking about their trusteeship of time and talent. But I am speaking to people who measure their property and time and talent in money more than anything else, and that is why I commend tithing to you.

May I offer a couple of observations from personal experience? One of them is that—and this is particularly for students and young married people—there will never come a "right" time to start tithing. The only way is to plunge right in where you are! There never comes a time when you have enough money or can afford to do it. It's not a spiritual exercise in responsibility, anyhow, if you give from what's left over after you've taken care of everything else your heart desires. The way to give is to take the 10 percent off the top of your income, not the bottom. By that I mean do it first, before you pay your expenses. It is a good deal like saving. For years we tried to save out of what was left over. We never saved much. (We still aren't endangering the Rockefellers any!) We never really began to save effectively at all until we took some bank's slogan to heart: "Pay yourself first." We get paid monthly, and we pay our bills monthly; when I sit down to write checks, I put the tithing accounts on top—church pledge, United Fund, and so on—and next after them the savings account book. It may not be true for you, but it is for us —the only way to save is to put some away first and live out of what's left; and the same is true of tithing.

In Philadelphia some years ago the annual Bok award was to be given to a citizen whose service was "best calculated to advance the best interests" of that distinguished community. The presentation took place before a large audience in the Academy of Music, and throughout the evening program suspense built up until the climactic secret was revealed. The time had come, and the master of ceremonies said that the award was going to "a great businessman." Then he pointed out that there are "two kinds of businesses, at least. There is a little business that uses men to make money." And "there is the big business," represented by the winner of the award that year: Rufus Jones, the Quaker philosopher and practical statesman who "uses money to make men and, when they are broken, to mend them." Surely that is our business—to use our time and talent and money—to make men and, when they are broken, to mend them! And the businesslike way to do it is by tithing.

Tithing has a way of helping us get the proper perspective on things. The late Edward R. Murrow of radio and TV fame was the son of a laboring man. A few years before his death Murrow was on his way to the Orient and stopped off to see his father, who was then a paralyzed invalid. A national magazine had recently carried a story on Murrow and had pointed out that he was one of the highest paid men in the industry, making over a quarter of a million dollars a year. His father, having seen the story, said, "I read where you make a right smart lot of money, son." "I guess that's right, Dad," he answered. "Well," the older man went on to say, "I wouldn't go so far as to say that it was downright dishonest, but it seems a little strange to me that you should get paid so much for just talking, especially when you don't make any better sense than I used to hear around the potbelly stove in the general store!" I know very little more about the elder Murrow than that, but he gives every indication of being a man who had a pretty sound perspective on things, the kind of perspective that tithing helps to give.

At one time during the Civil War the fighting swept through a little southern town. During the melee an old lady rushed out of her house, brandishing a broom handle as a weapon. A young soldier yelled, "Grandma, you can't fight with that!" But without hesitating she shot back, "I can show which side I'm on!" That is what I am really asking you to do. Some of us are able to do abundantly more than others; a few of us can do very little. But every last one of us can stir what he's got by tithing and thus show which side he's on!

Don't Cut the Buttons Off!

A while back a friend of mine was one of a group pack-
ing clothing contributed for overseas relief. Many of the
things were of good quality, in good repair, and had a
lot of use left in them; but it made him a little sad to
note that some of the clothing was hardly worth sending
—it was ragged and torn and needed mending. But the
saddest thing of all, he said later, was that some people
had cut all the buttons off the clothing they had given!
Can you imagine some thin and hungry refugee trying
to keep out the bitter cold of winter with a coat that has
no buttons? Or can you see him in your mind's eye trying to work in a pair of pants that he has to hold up
with one hand?

Perhaps we ought not to make too much of it.
Maybe the donors thought that their material would
only be used for rags or reprocessed in some way. Or
maybe it was only that some thrifty housewife, without
thinking, in an overzealous moment trimmed off the
buttons to save for use in repairing some other garment.

But, on the other hand, this may have been one of
those unconsciously revealing actions which "speak
louder than words." The psychologists say that we do
few things accidentally or thoughtlessly, that most such

lapses and slips reveal our deeper selves. How instinctively we hold on to what we have! How reluctantly do we part with anything we may be able to use! It is certainly true that much giving is grudging. So often we cut the buttons off our generosity! How often we have been guilty of

The organized charity, scrimped and iced,
In the name of a cautious, statistical Christ!

So let's not take that person who cut the buttons off as some kind of horrible example, but as someone pretty much like ourselves when it comes to the voluntary support of worthy causes. Let's turn the light of Christian stewardship on our own lives for a few moments.

I

We begin by trying to answer a natural question. What's wrong with cutting the buttons off? What's wrong with the thoughtless or even grudging giving that is characteristic of us all too often? For one thing, *it is petty, ignoble, small.* It is not the kind of thing that we associate with largeness of character. For example, I doubt if anyone would cut the buttons off a coat he was giving if he thought any of his friends would know he had done it. Why? Because he would know, deep down inside, that it's something less than a wholeheartedly generous thing to do. Shame may not be the loftiest of motivations, but the test of publicity is still one of the rules of thumb for knowing what's right. Would anyone want his picture in the paper cutting off buttons? Would any-one want to receive an award as the smallest giver of the year or for cutting off the most buttons from clothing for refugees? Life is too short to be little, and grudging giving is about as small as one can get. I don't know who it was that defined a gentleman as "one who tries to put back more than he takes out," but I think he was on the right track.

Why not cut the buttons off? For another thing, *it won't get the job done that needs to be done.* Neither Christianity nor freedom is going to win the world by halfhearted gestures, makeshift arrangements of "too little and too late." One of the winners of the Nobel Peace Prize in 1946 was John R. Mott, the missionary statesman and ecumenical pioneer. In the early years of this century he said that we could either send a thousand missionaries to Japan at once or send a million soldiers later. We know now how right he was. Oh, we didn't do it deliberately as much as we did it by just cutting the buttons off our giving, by giving so gingerly that we could never do more than a makeshift job of preaching the gospel either here or there. The same tide of fanatic nationalism that was rising then in Japan is rising in a dozen places today; is there any real reason to think that it will turn out differently if we go on in the same old way?

Cutting the buttons off our giving will not get the job done that has to be done in a local church either. One of the hard things to try to get across the edge of many pulpits these days is that the church is not "sitting pretty" without a care in the world. Imagine trying to convince people that more money is needed for local work when they are sitting in air-conditioned comfort on upholstered pews! Imagine trying to convince people who have built new plants and dedicated them debt-free within a few years that they need to give more generously! But that is the sobering fact. In many a church the number of persons willing and able to make unusually large contributions has steadily diminished. The tax situation being what it is, we are not likely to see their kind again. The result is that we need a great many more people who will give regularly and sacrificially of their more modest means. The result is that many of the persons who have given regularly to the church for years need to learn that nominal giving on their part will no longer get the job done.

I recently had occasion to look over some of the sermons preached by Harry Emerson Fosdick at the famous Riverside Church in New York City. Imagine my surprise to find that twenty-five or thirty years ago they were facing this same problem of replacing a decreasing number of large givers by multiplying the giving from those of more moderate means! In one sermon he told about a man who after years spent dodging New York City traffic whimsically said that if he were ever "bumped off," an appropriate epitaph would be, "Died of looking the wrong way"! So we may say that if serious financial problems hit the American churches, it will be death "from looking the wrong way"—from depending too much on the large gifts of a few rather than the personal and sacrificial involvement of many.

But the most important reason of all for not cutting the buttons off is that *to do so takes all the fun out of giving.* There's no joy or satisfaction in giving that way. The Bible tells us that "God loves a cheerful giver" (II Cor. 9:7). I guess we all know why. So does everyone else! But does anyone love the man who's got the first nickel he ever made? The biggest trouble with grudging giving is not what it reveals nor even what happens to the recipient nor the cause, but what happens to the giver: He soon is a specimen of what someone has called "sour godliness."

A sportswriter once said of Willie Mays that he "plays baseball with a boy's glee, a pro's sureness, and a champion's flair." There is always something of glee and of flair about a champion—a gusto, an illimitable joy. One of the men who knew Babe Ruth intimately and followed his whole career says that "one of the secrets of the Babe's greatness was that he never lost his enthusiasm for playing ball, and especially for hitting home runs . . . whether . . . in a regular game, a World Series game, or an exhibition game." It seems to me that it's a good deal like that in Christian stewardship; the people I have known who have been champions at it never lose their enthusiasm for giving, but those who have made a habit of cutting the buttons off always seem to be on the grim and dissatisfied and unhappy side. And I suspect that here, as with almost everything else, what we do tends to determine what we are.

Don't cut the buttons off! Why? Because it's cheap

and little, it won't get the job done, and it takes all the fun out of giving.

II

It is always easy to analyze and to criticize what's wrong. It's not as easy to say what's right. If grudging giving doesn't fill the bill of Christian stewardship, what does? The answer can be put in one sentence. *Stewardship of possessions means that the tithe is the minimum standard of giving for Christians.* Tithing means giving 10 percent of one's personal or family income. I would like to stop right there, but you know as well as I that whenever the subject of tithing is mentioned, certain familiar flags are run to the top of the pole, and everyone chooses a position he is prepared to defend to the death. I do not want to argue with anyone about it. I only want to bear my witness by confessing to some things that bother me.

One of the things that bothers me when tithing is under discussion is for people to spend their time framing objections to it. I have heard it called hard and legalistic. It can be termed unfair because 10 percent of a $3,000 income is really a greater sacrifice than 10 percent of a $10,000 income. It can be said that there are weightier matters to the Christian life. It can be said that some people give a great deal of time and therefore ought not to be expected to give as much money as others. And so on. These objections disturb me because they seem usually to be defense mechanisms triggered in minds already determined to excuse themselves for

28

not giving 10 percent. They are heard more frequently from those with good incomes than from those with poor incomes. The only answer I can give is that once one tries tithing they seem to be irrelevant.

Another thing that bothers me when tithing is under discussion is for someone, usually with the best of intentions, to testify that if one will only tithe, an almost magical sort of blessing and reward will come to him. I have heard scores of stories of people who were practically down-and-out until they began to tithe; then things began to go their way, and now they live on easy street. I do not question their sincerity; I do question the closeness of the cause-and-effect relationship.

Some years ago after the Giants had won the World Series, one of the players on the team was talking to a Sunday school class about tithing. One of the class members asked him whether he thought that his tithing had had anything to do with the success of his team in the Series. The player had to remind him that he had been a tither with two teams that had lost the Series, and then he went on to say, "Whether we win or lose, I'll still be tithing." I do not know if he has kept to that, but I suspect he has even though it was public knowledge within a few years that his personal fortunes had taken a turn for the worse. For his name was Alvin Dark, and he was ingloriously fired as a major league manager. God is not some sort of glorified vending machine that reacts with a trinket when we put in the right coin!

I think that many get more joy and satisfaction out of the 90 percent they spend on themselves when they give

10 percent because they have the joy that comes from generosity, and they are better managers of the 90 percent than they were of the 100 percent before. But you will not hear it from me, even by implication, that financial success and earthly blessings will come your way if you only tithe.

Most of all I am bothered by those who think a tither has taken care of his obligations as a Christian steward. This is where a hard and altogether unlovely smugness and complacency all too easily appear. So I must say it again. Tithing is the *minimum* standard. Many, perhaps most, of us in our "affluent society" ought to give *more* than that. A Christian steward never gets to the place where he can complacently rest on his oars, saying, "I've done my share." There always rings too loudly in his ears the Master's word, "When you have done all that is commanded . . . say, 'We are unworthy servants; we have only done what was our duty' " (Luke 17:10).

One of the classic illustrations of what I am saying is John Wesley's example as a student at Oxford. The noted reformer describes a member of the Holy Club in the third person, but he is speaking about himself:

One of them had thirty pounds a year. He lived on twenty-eight, and gave away forty shillings. The next year receiving sixty pounds, he still lived on twenty-eight, and gave away two and thirty. The third year he received ninety pounds, and gave away sixty-two. The fourth year he received a hundred and twenty pounds. Still he lived as before on twenty-eight and gave to the poor ninety-two.

I do not suppose that he lived all his life on twenty-eight pounds a year. But I do know that he *never* thought that he had arrived and no longer needed to grow in giving or in any other aspect of the Christian life. He took tithing as a minimum goal, but when he got there he didn't stop.

My plea then is simple. If you are not a tither, I ask you to reexamine your giving and take a significant step toward tithing this very month. If you are a tither, I ask you to consider whether or not you ought to be growing even further.

III

Perhaps the best way to put it is this: giving 10 percent, or more, is *something you owe to yourself.* Someone asked Boris Pasternak why he wrote his Nobel prize–winning, runaway best seller, *Dr. Zhivago.* The Russian author was fully aware that his theme could hardly be popular in the Kremlin; when he could not get it published in his own country, he knew that he was risking at the least a campaign of vilification against himself and perhaps his very life and the future of his family to allow its publication abroad. Yet he went ahead. Why? "I said to myself, you must stand up straight before your own name." It is about tithing as a way of meeting that inner obligation, as a way of standing up straight before one's own name, that I am writing.

Let me state then a perfectly simple and self-evident

fact, yet one which we commonly overlook: *we are all debtors*. As F. W. Boreham once put it,

We began early. When making our preparations for invading this planet, we naturally came to the conclusion that our equipment would be lamentably incomplete unless we brought a body with us. But a body was the one thing that we did not happen to possess. A body is composed of certain chemical substances. It consists of so much iron, so much phosphate, so much salt, so much soda. . . . We could not very well begin without a body: a body required all these substances: and we did not chance to have any of them. . . . What could we do?

Borrowing was inevitable. But from whom? It is begging the issue to say that we borrowed from our parents. They no more possessed these chemical ingredients in their own right than we did. If they had them, it was because they themselves had borrowed them. . . . Strictly speaking, therefore, it was from the earth that we borrowed them.

The same thing holds true wherever we turn. We are debtors not merely to mother earth for our bodies, but to the parents who nurtured and protected our personalities and characters. We are all debtors to that incredibly long line of persons who have labored for the education of the race. One of the characters in the comic strip "Peanuts" once loudly proclaimed, "I'm self-educated! I don't need teachers! I don't need schools! I don't need books!" So Charlie Brown asked the secret of such success, and the answer came back complete with an oratorical flourish, "Everything I've learned I've learned from watching TV!"

And when you come right down to it, what of the wood in our homes? However high the price of lumber and however high the lumbermen are paid, there is still a balance owing. What of the soldiers and sailors who hazard their lives in our defense, and what of the high-minded statesmen held by a sense of duty to the leadership of our nation? Do we dispose of our obligations to them by paying our taxes? The shallowness of that answer was never made more plain than when Frank Costello, the underworld czar, was asked what he had done during the war for the country he was claiming as his. The only answer he could muster was, "I paid my taxes"! We are all debtors! How different from Frank Costello was Albert Einstein, who once confessed, "A hundred times a day I remind myself that my inner and outer life depend on the labors of other men, living and dead, and that I must exert myself in order to give in the same measure as I have received and am receiving." It was not some flight of fancy rhetoric, but a simple statement of fact when Paul had the sensitivity to write that he was "under obligation both to Greeks and to barbarians, both to the wise and to the foolish" (Rom. 1:14). So are we all.

That being so, let us note that *most of us do better at meeting our obligations when we make regular payments.* Most of us would never repay in a lifetime a $15,000 or $20,000 loan to build a house; but when we have regular payments to meet, we get it done in twenty years. I know a man who is far more self-disciplined than most when it comes to resisting what Dr. Robert Hutchins wryly dubbed "our new way of getting rich" —"which is to buy things from one another that we do not want at prices we cannot pay on terms we cannot meet because of advertising we do not believe." But this man has often bought things "on time" when he had the cash in the bank to pay for them. Why? "Because," he once said, "I find it a good way to make myself save."

Most of us do better when we make regular payments, I suppose, partly because it puts a goal before us. Every salesman knows that he does better when he has a quota to meet. There is a stimulus in a deadline. Even creative artists find it necessary to write so many words a day or put in so many hours at the easel. In the state of Washington it is rumored that the state police officers have a quota of so many arrests per day. Anyone can see the undesirable features of such a system—patrolmen "straining at gnats" when short an arrest or two for the day or "swallowing camels" once they have met their quota. And suppose there should be a day when there just weren't enough traffic violations for every man on duty to get his quota! And yet there is a streak of carelessness, of laziness, or of something else in most of us —and police officers are no exception—which tends to drag our performance down if we do not have at least minimum standards to meet.

Then again we do better when we make regular payments because it is psychologically and physiologically true that every time we do something we make it easier to do the same thing again. Somewhere deep within our cells, our nerve endings, our chemical molecules, every action traces its path, leaves its tiny mark. The more frequently and regularly anything is done, the broader these "highways of habit" become until we can do some things, as we say, "by second nature" or "in our sleep." Hence, wrote William James, the pioneer psychologist, "Sow an action and you reap a habit; sow a habit and you reap a character; sow a character and you reap a destiny."

So with our payments on our indebtedness to the Author and Giver of life. We all have moments when we feel deeply grateful; we all have moments of high resolve when we intend to make a *real* payment. But most of us do a lot better over the long pull if we just put aside 10 percent, or more, regularly "for the work of the Lord." If you will do that and if you will put your church pledge on top of the pile when you write your checks to pay monthly bills, I can guarantee from personal experience that you will both do better and feel better about what you have done.

To draw an example from a wholly nonecclesiastical source, let us turn to the world of the theater. People in show business, with more than a little justification, often look upon the professional critics almost as enemies. But some time ago many of the top stars of the theater gave a surprise party for Brooks Atkinson, who was about to retire from the *New York Times.* There were "command performances" and gifts and speeches. Finally, of course, he had to make some response. He only spoke for two minutes, but the gist of the attitude which had made him the "dean of U. S. drama critics" came through in just eight words: "I have tried to be on the level." That is stewardship! And that is why I plead, don't cut the buttons off!

The Arrest of Papa Dio

Several years ago the New York narcotics squad raided a loft apartment in one of the depressed areas of the city. "Every square foot of the long, dingy apartment was crowded with human derelicts who were sleeping on the floor, or sitting huddled in corners"; dimly visible overhead were a number of fading paper ornaments, hangovers from the days when the loft had been a gaily decorated dance hall. After searching everyone, the detectives arrested six men who were carrying hypodermic needles and packets of heroin. They also arrested a man who readily admitted being in charge, the host to all the others—a mild-mannered seedy-looking sort of fellow.

At headquarters the seedy-looking fellow was booked on a charge of harboring drug addicts in his apartment. Asked who he was, he identified himself as John Sargent Cram and claimed to be a millionaire who had been educated at Princeton and Oxford. He had chosen to live among the homeless, he said, in order to give them at least the minimum essentials in the way of food, clothing, and shelter. He made it a point not to give any of them money because he had found that it almost always went for cheap wine, but his door was open to all, including the small minority of drug addicts, because he had not known that it was against the law to feed and clothe such people.

Checking his story, the police found it to be true. Wishing to avoid the fanfare and red tape of organized charities, Cram had simply moved into a loft and set about doing what he could personally and directly, at a cost of about one hundred dollars a day. When his case came up for a hearing, a number of witnesses testified to his kindness and altruism, and it was brought out that the Spanish-speaking population of the area knew him as Papa Dio—Father God. Amid their cheers he was freed on his promise not to harbor any more drug addicts, and, so far as I know, he is still carrying on his own personal brand of philanthropy.

There are a lot of angles on a story like this which rouse curiosity. The connoisseur of Americana would see in the story another man to add to a notable line of eccentrics whose oddball individualism we like to cherish as something that could happen "only in America." The Internal Revenue Service, I suppose, would be interested in determining how much Cram had been deducting as contributions to charity, and might even ask him to file itemizations for all expenditures over twenty-five dollars. Former Senator Goldwater would doubtless see in it a fine example of rugged individualism and personal initiative, while the advocates of the Great Society would more likely emphasize the need it demonstrates for a war on poverty. Some state legislators might find in it adequate justification for their skepticism about the real values of investing more money in higher education—any man who had been to Princeton and Oxford and had ended up doing something like that with his money obviously hadn't developed fiscal responsibility! Since Cram's activities were in a Spanish-speaking neighborhood, they might even reward investigation as a center of Cuban refugee activity on the one hand or as an incipient infection of Castro communism on the other. Any preacher worth his salt ought to be able to see many parallels with Jesus' story of the Good Samaritan.

But the recurring question it stirred in my mind was this: Why would somebody do something like that? Why would a person who was well-to-do invest the income from a million dollars *plus* his own time in living with and helping people whom he did not know and with whom he had very little in common?

I

The first answer I thought of was that *maybe he was doing it out of a sense of guilt*. There are a lot of people who give primarily from that motivation. They give only when they are made to feel that they ought to, when they are shamed into it, so to speak. They remind me a little of a story about the Senator who at the age of ninety was still in office. He was a wealthy man but also one who had reputation for penny-pinching. A reporter once asked one of the Senator's office aides why someone hadn't pointed out to him that he wasn't going to be able to take his money with him. To which the aide replied, "Why, we can't even persuade him that someday he will have to go."

It didn't take me long to throw out the idea of Cram's giving simply from feelings of guilt. Mr. Cram had no particular and immediate responsibility, nothing that could make him do what he was doing, no enforceable obligation. He didn't show any signs of guilt feelings. Of course, in both democratic sociology and in Protestant Christian theology we are all responsible for one another and have a duty to help whoever needs what we can supply, but that's entirely too theoretical and idealistic to be an explanation for his actions.

Another answer I thought of was that *maybe he was doing it because he felt sorry for them;* maybe like the Samaritan he had "compassion" (Luke 10:33). That is surely a worthy motive for giving, and there are a good many people who are responsive to it. When they see a stark human need, they impulsively want to do something about it.

One of the men who accompanied Franklin D. Roosevelt on his first campaign for the presidency told how he remembered their visit to Chicago and how horrified he was to see people sleeping under the bridges; he remarked to the candidate that it was a funny place for a man to sleep, and Roosevelt answered: "Well, he doesn't sleep there; he lives there. And he's lucky if he can get enough to eat there to be able to stay on instead of falling into the river." Most of us, I suspect, if personally and directly confronted with stark, elemental human need like that would be moved to do something about it. We don't want to be taken for suckers, and we don't want to encourage free-loading, but I doubt if there's a single one of us who wouldn't be moved to do something for a person who was really up against it through no fault of his own. In fact, most of us are actually giving through our United Fund and through our churches for the alleviation of just such human misery.

But at best I think we would all agree that even compassion doesn't fully unravel the mystery of Papa Dio's giving. There was something less noble, perhaps, but more elemental about it than that.

II

Perhaps the clue to his behavior was given in an interview he had with reporters after his case had been dismissed. "I don't know that my work does much good," he said, "but I don't think it does any harm. . . . I'm quite happy, you know. I'm anything but a despondent person. Call me eccentric. Call it my reason for being. I have no other."

He was giving so unreservedly of his money and himself because *it filled an inner need of his own being,* it provided a "reason for being"—a justification to himself for his own existence. We all need to be needed! (One of the big Detroit auto companies did some motivational research on why people bought Volkswagens. "That's easy," replied one VW owner, "it needs me.")

He was giving that way because it gave his own life

meaning and purpose beyond itself; it saved him from being helplessly imprisoned by his money and his society; it saved him from pressures and ulcers and tensions—"I'm quite happy, you know." It gave him a rare freedom from most of the problems that bedevil many of us, and I suspect that deep down inside more than one of us think that doing something like that makes a lot more sense than we would be willing to let on. It's not something that everyone could do, of course; it won't serve as a pattern for social work or reform; it is full of all kinds of impracticalities even if we had the million dollars—which most of us don't. But there is something winsome and attractive about it all the same, and my guess is that this "something" is related to the triviality and superficiality of much of our lives.

Most of us would like to do something enduringly useful and be someone of lasting, genuine worth—the kind of person that others spontaneously recognize as the salt of the earth. But we don't quite dare let ourselves go; we are inhibited by doubts and fears and insecurities; we rationalize to ourselves a thousand good reasons why we do what we do; we drive ourselves in a whirlwind of professional and civic and church activities; we punish our bodies with psychosomatic troubles. We long for an image of being useful, generous, unselfish, but we always hold back at the crucial juncture with the result that our work turns out to be a skirting of the fringes rather than a satisfying involvement in the center.

III

What the Bible offers as a practical remedy to our situation was suggested by a cartoon which showed a number of businessmen at a conference table; one was saying, "What we need is a brand new idea that has been thoroughly tested." Christianity offers exactly that to meet this inner need of our own being. *It is called tithing.* It is one of the most thoroughly tested ideas in the religious life; it has been a help to people for at least three or four thousand years. Yet it is one which is new to each generation and one whose satisfactions must be personally experienced to be understood.

This inner need within each of us to give—as the story of the arrest of Papa Dio suggests and as Jesus noted when he said that it makes one happier to give than to receive (Acts 20:35)—explains much of our anxiety. We are cursed with the curses (Mal. 3:9) of unhappiness and insecurity because we don't give enough to meet our own inner need; we starve and strangle and suffocate an impulse which we ought to express gladly and freely. The latest figures I have seen on our giving to Protestant churches, for example, show that we give about a tithe of the income of a couple living on social security! This figure is even more startling when held up against another I came on quite by accident: "A research organization has announced that the cash lost each year in the United States amounts to about $75 per capita. By 'lost' the research people don't mean bad luck in business investments or bingo or poker or the horses. They use the word 'lost' literally; that is, money that falls out of pockets or that is in wallets or purses which are misplaced, etc." We *lose* more money, on the average, than we *give!*

I know it sounds corny, but I am persuaded that this question says something we need to hear: Are you living more but enjoying it less? Try tithing. The ancient Jewish standard was a tenth; the modern affluent American Christian is not likely to find satisfaction in anything less, and probably should be giving a good deal more.

IV

Let's move on, therefore, to look a little more closely at what tithing does for us, at how this way of giving meets the fundamental needs of our natures. For one thing, *giving this way helps us to stay alive and growing.* A tree, although it must have water to live, cannot stay alive simply by receiving water. It must give away gallons of it every day through its leaves. If in some way a tree should stop giving, it would also stop growing and would soon die.

It seems to be a basic principle that you have to give in order to receive. It's as true of a man as of a tree. Do you remember how that dried-up, shriveled old miser Silas Marner came alive when his hoard of gold was stolen and a golden-haired baby, who demanded time and attention and money, came into his life instead?

One of the best "dissertations" on the subject of giving and receiving is found on a scrap of paper mounted behind glass in a desert store in southern California. It was written with a stub of a pencil on a piece of wrapping paper which had originally been folded and put into a baking powder can. The battered can had been wired to an old pump which offered the only chance of water on a long and seldom used trail across the desert. The message went like this:

This pump is all right as of June, 1932. I put a new sucker washer into it and it ought to last five years. But the washer dries out and the pump has got to be primed. Under the white rock I buried a bottle of water, out of the sun and cork end up. There's enough water in it to prime this pump but not if you drink some first. Pour in about one-fourth and let her soak to wet the leather. Then pour in the rest medium fast and pump like hell. You'll git water. The well never has run dry. Have faith. When you get watered up, fill the bottle and put it back like you found it for the next feller.

(signed) *Desert Pete*

P. S. Don't go drinking the water first. Prime the pump with it and you'll git all you can hold. And next time you pray, remember that God is like this pump. He has to be primed. I've give my last dime away a dozen times to prime the pump of my prayer, and I've fed my last beans to a stranger while saying Amen. It never failed yet to git me an answer. You got to git your heart fixed to give before you can be give to.

Pete

"You got to git your heart fixed to give before you can be give to"—you have to give in order to receive, in order to stay alive and growing.

Bishop Gerald Kennedy once said, "The strong must bear the burdens of the weak not for the sake of the weak but for the sake of the strong." At first this statement puzzled me, but the more I think about it, the more I see how true it is. If a person is to stay alive and growing, he must continually give of his health and strength, or God quietly and unobtrusively takes them from him. J. C. Furnas in his book *Goodbye to Uncle Tom* points out that one of the most insidious evils of the slave system, as recognized by sensitive Americans and by foreign visitors alike, was its degrading effect upon the master and his children. They were always on the receiving end, and in the words of Jefferson, "The man must be a prodigy who can retain his manners and his morals undepraved by such circumstances." The law of Christ that we "bear one another's burdens" (Gal. 6:2) is for the benefit not only of the weak but also the strong. The giver needs to give in order to satisfy the hunger of his own being to stay alive and growing.

Then again, tithing enables us *to share in achieving the goals and values we respect.* There is really little genuine satisfaction to be gained from something if we have not given of ourselves to help bring it about.

Leslie Weatherhead once told about hearing the conversation of two dear old English ladies. As one poured tea by their comfortable little fire, the other opened the daily paper, which was full of news of World War II. Presently she said, "I see *we've* taken Tobruk." By an extension of her own personality she felt herself a part of the fighting forces of Great Britain. They both spoke feelingly of "our" men and what "we've" accomplished. Was this identification of themselves with the life of their nation in its epic fight against tyranny mere comfortable fantasy? Not necessarily; not if they had given a son or a grandson to the cause; not even if they had personally queued up in a line uncomplainingly to buy their rationed tea; not if they had paid their share of the war taxes. By giving of themselves they had a right to share in the goals being accomplished.

Here, as I see it, is one of the strong reasons why each of us should have a part in United Fund community appeals. The individual organizations may not all be of concern to us, but if we want the full satisfaction of living in a town with a strong community consciousness, we have to give to get it! If we want the satisfaction of encouraging what *Time* magazine recently called "the general change in business philosophy" which makes the businessman responsible not only for products and payrolls, but also for the social well-being of the market he serves, we have to give to get it!

Do you remember how Aaron tried to excuse himself to Moses? He had yielded in Moses' absence to the pressure to make a golden idol for the people to worship. Now he was confronting the stern desert lawmaker: "You know the people, that they are set on evil. For they said to me, 'Make us gods.' . . . And I said to them, 'Let

47

any who have gold take it off'; so they gave it to me, and I threw it into the fire, and there came out this calf" (Exod. 32:22b-23a, 24) . He was trying to say that he was not responsible, and there are plenty of his descendants today who shirk responsibility! But they also lose the satisfaction of sharing in the achievement of goals they respect.

Someone has said, "Sour godliness is the devil's religion." You know the type: people who have so repressed and dried up their impulses to give that their lives have become sour and bitter; even their religion makes them miserable because they miss the joy and satisfaction of sharing in the achievement of goals they grudgingly must respect.

Finally, *giving 10 percent or more meets our need to give an account of ourselves.* Sensitive people always seem to feel that there is an "ought" to life, that they are accountable somewhere, someday, for what they've done with themselves. It's a feeling that people get in every area of life. Upon returning from a tour of the Far East, the U. S. pianist Eugene Istomin began preparing for another world tour. Asked when he was going to settle down and accept some of the less strenuous offers here at home (he played with the Philadelphia Orchestra and the New York Philharmonic when he was only seventeen) , he replied that he had a duty to perform. He pointed out that he had been trained under the influence of the wartime influx of great European artists like Rubinstein, Schnabel, and Walter. "I felt as though artistically I had robbed the city bank of New York." So he says, "We have an obligation to pass that on to other parts of the world. It's a way of paying back what we have borrowed."

All of us begin on borrowed capital. We brought nothing into the world. Through the years, if we are decent, we try in some measure to give an account of ourselves to our parents and teachers and friends from whom we borrow experience, examples, and courage so heavily. Shall we not then render some reckoning to the Author and Giver of life itself? Or shall we be like the drunken sailor who was hailed before the judge? His honor inquired what had happened to the sailor's money. "Well," came the unsteady explanation, "I spent some on liquor, and some on women, and the rest foolishly."

The need of the giver to give is rooted in his own sense of accountability. Jesus says relatively little about giving but a great deal about accountability. He would have concurred in Abraham Lincoln's stately dictum: "I hold that while man exists it is his duty to improve not only his own condition but to assist in ameliorating mankind." The crucial reason for Christian giving is a sense of responsibility to God for the right use of all we have. As the psalmists put it, "It is he that hath made us and not we ourselves" (Ps. 100:3 KJV). It is he "who gives . . . power to get wealth" (Deut. 8:18) and everything else. If we give because of the "need" of the church or to meet the budget or to complete our building projects, we miss the real point and, more than likely, the real happiness.

Hi-fi phonographs were all the rage when they first

came out. Well, high fidelity has been the code of the Christian from the start. Faithfulness in reproducing in our lives the living accents of the Most High is our supreme obligation. Unless a man is faithful in the use of what he has, says Jesus, "even what he has will be taken away" (Matt. 25:29). A man needs to give "as God hath prospered him" (I Cor. 16:2 KJV) in order to render a faithful account of himself.

Since Bible times there has stood one great symbol of man's responsibility to God, one great satisfaction for the hunger-to-give: the giving of 10 percent or more of one's income. We have not always been very articulate about tithing as a Christian grace. We know full well the dangers of a hard and unlovely legalism. But surely we ought not to give less from our abundance than the poorest Jew was expected to give from his poverty! I believe that tithing works—that once people give it a genuine trial they are never again satisfied with their old ways of giving. So my suggestion is simple: "Step up" to tithing for one month as a trial; give it the test of your own experience!

There is a revealing story told of a wealthy man who had never been what anyone would call a generous giver. His church was having a big expansion program and financial campaign so they resolved to visit him, nevertheless. In order to succeed where they had so often failed, they appointed a committee to study the situation. Finally the committee called on the prospect and told him that in view of his resources they were sure that he would want to make a rather substantial contribution. "I see," he said, "that you have considered it all quite carefully. In the course of your investigation did you discover that I have an aged, widowed mother who has no other means of support?" No, they hadn't known that. "Did you know that I have a sister who was left by a drunken husband with five small children and no means of providing for them?" No, they hadn't known that. "Did you know that I have a brother who was crippled in an accident and will never be able to do another day's work in his life to support himself and his family?" No, they hadn't known that. "Well," he thundered triumphantly, "I've never done anything for them, so why should I do anything for you?" Why? Simply because a man needs to keep alive and growing, because he needs to have a share in the achievement of goals he respects, and because he needs to give an account of himself to the One on whose capital he began.

The Best of All Investments

Few living Americans have had as long and varied experience in politics as Joe Martin of Massachusetts, who held a political position until he was in his eighties. For twenty years he was Republican Leader in the House of Representatives, and twice Speaker of that body. He was a convention floor manager for presidential hopefuls, permanent chairman of five national conventions, and chairman of his party's National Committee. For eighteen months, as Speaker, he was the designated successor to the President, there being no Vice-President—a heart beat away from the highest office in the land. Veteran Washington observers and correspondents say that no member of Congress was better liked or more thoroughly trusted by his colleagues of both parties. His Democratic opposite, Sam Rayburn, once said, "When you make an agreement with Joe Martin you don't have to remember it, because he will." He has known the bitter as well as the sweet, however. His party was out of power during much of his career. Step by step he worked his way from the obscurity of a freshman legislator to the leadership, only to be publicly rebuffed a few years before his enforced retirement by the selection of another Minority Leader, thus reducing him to the obscurity of the back row.

In *My First Fifty Years in Politics* he shares in his

own warm, direct, and unassuming way anecdotes and observations on practically every major political figure and issue of this century and passes along some of the lessons he has learned from them. He closes the book with this statement: "After years of living with the coldest realities I still believe that one reaps what one sows and that to sow kindness is the best of all investments."

To sow kindness is the best of all investments! This is a modern version of what we read in Ecclesiastes, "Cast your bread upon the waters, for you will find it after many days" (11:1), and it is a direct reference to Paul's word that "he who sows sparingly will also reap sparingly, and he who sows bountifully will also reap bountifully" (II Cor. 9:6). We may forget that the writers of scripture, for the most part, were hardheaded, practical men; but no one of us will accuse a professional, lifelong politician, who had no formal education beyond the high school level and no family wealth or prestige to trade on, of being too idealistic! So his word comes to us with considerable authority; the peculiarly practical authority of the voice of experience, the authority of one in the twilight of his career who has no ax —religious, political, economic, or other—to grind: "I ... believe that one reaps what one sows and that to sow kindness is the best of all investments."

I

First of all, then, let us note the obvious: *to sow kindness is clearly the best of all investments for the world in general.* There isn't a problem before us as a society, from taxes to Vietnam, which wouldn't be eased by kindness all around; there isn't a spot of friction in the world, from domestic spats to Red China, that wouldn't be eased by the oil of kindness.

We spent a summer in Alaska one year, and there I learned about a man named William Duncan. He first came as a missionary to an island with the unlikely name of Metlakatla. The Indians were an ignorant, generally miserable, poverty-stricken, and uncivilized lot when he arrived. But a man who visited the same island a few years after William Duncan had lived and labored there reported that he found every family living in a decent home and that Metlakatla had acquired a bank, sawmill, store, box factory, and salmon cannery run by the Indians themselves in sober and profitable industry. There was a school and a church under the leadership of native sons. And it was all as a direct result of William Duncan's work of sowing Christian kindness!

Stand the principle on its head for a moment. Does anyone think that our best hope is to sow brutality? Joseph Stalin, Adolph Hitler, and Mao Tse-tung are the exponents of that philosophy! No, there is no question about it—as far as society is concerned Joe Martin is absolutely right: to sow kindness is the best of all investments.

II

In the second place, *the same thing is true for individuals.* Which, of course, is basically what Joe Martin was talking about; his experience had been that there was nothing better he could do for himself than to be kind to others; it was an investment that paid the biggest and most regular of all dividends.

A man by the name of Sam Reeve was invited a few years ago to a presidential White House Conference on small businesses. It was known that he had started twenty years before with $1.50 and that he had multiplied it into one of the largest service station businesses in the state of Michigan. The administration wanted to know how he had done it. His place of business was not exclusive—the other three corners of the intersection had stations as large and bright and carrying comparable quality merchandise. What was his secret? "I just tried to give away more than my competitors," he said. Stamps or prizes or chances on new cars? No. He gives away service. After every snowstorm he plows out hundreds of driveways free of charge. He will baby-sit with a youngster, pick up grocery orders, meet unexpected guests at the airport, or turn off house lights accidentally left burning, and never charge a dime! When an important Detroit executive visited him and asked him where he got the idea, Sam pointed to a dog-eared, scotch-taped Bible. "It belonged to my Dad," he said, "and I try to run this station by this passage: 'Give, and it shall be given unto you; good measure, pressed down, and shaken together, and running over. . . . For with the same measure that ye mete withal it shall be measured to you again'" (Luke 6:38 KJV). He had started by giving away free parking and free up-to-the-door delivery of workers' cars in bad weather, no strings attached. And now, twenty-five years later, he is still giving away free service. His investments in kindness have proved to be the best he's ever made.

III

In the third place, let me make a simple and direct statement. When your church asks for pledges to support its work, *you are asked to make a personal investment in kindness.* Before that time you will probably receive quite a bit of information through the mail and at church about the church and its program and the amounts necessary to sustain them. But as nearly as any one word can cover anything so complex, kindness sums up what the church means, what it believes in, what it tries to practice and extend throughout the world in both individual lives and social affairs. We serve a Lord who said that the final test was whether or not we gave food to the hungry, water to the thirsty, clothing to the naked, friendship to the friendless (Matt. 25:35-40) —whether or not we were *kind.* That is what church buildings are for, that is what local operating expenses are for, that is the purpose of all our benevolence!

As you think about your investment in kindness, will you heed a word from a spiritual counselor? Before making any other kind of investment, most of us seek the advice of a counselor in the field. The passage we have mentioned from Ecclesiastes, beginning, "Cast your bread upon the waters," Jewish scholar Robert Gordis tells us, really means: "Diversify your investments. Don't put all your eggs in one basket." May I ask you then to think about your investment portfolios—the places where you've been putting money: children, home, cars, savings, stocks, vacations, and all the rest—and see if you've been putting an adequate amount into kindness? There is one easy way to check: Are you putting 10 percent, a tithe, or more into the work of the Lord? If you are not giving 10 percent of your family income, will you thoughtfully and prayerfully consider it and decide how big a step you can take toward it this year? I am suggesting that you try investing 10 percent or more of your pay in kindness and see for yourself whether or not it pays big dividends!

IV

I am advising you to try tithing not only because it is biblical but also because the way we give says a good deal about us. "Money talks," as the saying goes. The way we handle it says a good deal about character, values, and goals. If you doubt that, in the privacy of your own home try reflectively going over your checkbook for the last year; what does it say about you? You remember Jesus' story of three employees who were entrusted by their boss with considerable amounts of money—five talents, two talents, one talent (which was still a sizable sum). What they did with that which was entrusted to them speaks volumes.

One thing it says is that *all three were prudent and reliable.* None of them lost the money through carelessness; none of them spent it unwisely; none of them lost it in gambling or drinking. They were all prudent and reliable men. The confidence of their master was not misplaced. When you've said that, you've said a good deal. How many of us have done as well? If we were called to render a strict account for the several thousand dollars that we handle each year, how would we stand up? My surmise is that we'd be amazed! Without decrying recreation—haven't you ever felt your money was wasted in a movie, or that in eating out you paid a good deal more than the meal was really worth?

Prudence and reliability come close to being the basic American virtues. The story goes that a pioneer was walking from his clearing to the meeting house, his trusty flintlock expertly balanced on his arm. A nonbeliever accosted him with the question, "Brother Nathan, is it not your belief that what is destined to be will be?" "Yes." "Then if all the Indians in the province attacked the meeting house and your time had not yet come, you would not be harmed?" "No." "But if your time had come," pursued the other with remorseless logic, "then no matter what you did, it would do no good?" "That is right." "Then why do you carry your gun to the meeting?" The grave reply was, "On my way I might see an Indian whose time had come." The way our pioneer fathers used their worldly goods shows that prudence and reliability were part of their being.

Another thing that the parable of the talents says, however, is that *you can be too prudent.* Undoubtedly the safest thing to do with the talent was to bury it; that policy involved the least risk. But it was not the one the master commended! You can be too prudent.

When the Washington monument was proposed, a well-to-do Virginia farmer bluntly refused any contribution, saying he needed no monument to remember Washington, for he had him always in his heart. Anyone who has ever solicited funds for any cause knows the type and rejoices in the answer the solicitor gave him, "All I can say, then, is that George Washington has gotten into a mighty tight place!" And, by the same token, Jesus Christ has known solitary confinement in the hearts of many who have been too prudent.

There is a time when courageous enterprise is the order of the day; to be found wanting then is to miss his kingdom's goal. Louis Nizer, the distinguished New York lawyer whose book *My Life in Court* was high on the best seller lists for many months, gives a fascinating account of a proxy fight for the control of a large corporation. He attributes to Napoleon a dictum about the three things "necessary to win a war: money, money, money." The church is involved in a never ending warfare far more extensive than any of Napoleon's or Mr. Nizer's—the battle against wrong, injustice, evil, ignorance, and disease on every front. It is in conflict with the more subtle cancers of arrogance, atheism, and idolatry. And it will never win by being too prudent.

A third thing that the parable says is that *it is the enterprising, not the fearful, who are worthy of a higher responsibility.* "You have been faithful over a little, I will set you over much" (Matt. 25:23) . The importance of this lies in the fact that the good life is made up of a succession of higher and higher responsibilities. Growing up is a process of preparation for higher responsibilities. Marriage is a process of higher responsibilities. Civilization is a process of higher and higher responsibilities. Christianity sets forth the highest responsibility conceivable in the mind of man: "You, therefore, must be perfect, as your heavenly Father is perfect" (Matt. 5:48). We are creatures so made as to grow and thrive and mature on responsibility.

Even in childhood the desire to have goals and to reach new levels of responsibility is evident. It was Roger's first day at kindergarten, and he wandered around examining the low tables and chairs, the cupboards with coat hooks just his height, even the washroom where everything was scaled to five-year-old size. Finally he walked up to the teacher and announced, "I don't like it here. There's nothing to grow up to." Somehow, I do not fear for the future of that kind of boy! I suspect that a part of the problem of a good many of us is that we are no longer responding to life's challenge to grow up. We think we have. We think we've arrived. But if we have, we're dead, whether our name has been in the obituary column or not. Only to the enterprising does additional responsibility go!

There is yet another thing the parable says to us: *each person bears an individual responsibility.* When the employer came back, he didn't add up all the receipts and divide by three to get an average—he took each one separately on his own performance. That is what any normal businessman does. There is something very pertinent here for our American way of life in general, and the financing of the church in particular. The tendency of our time is toward obscuring individual responsibility. We worship at the feet of the general average. We divide the gross national product by the population and get an average income, or average productivity, or average something else. On the average it often looks as though a church is doing pretty well. But the average is misleading; a relatively small number of families who tithe substantial incomes may hide the fact that many families are not giving in proportion to their ability at all! Every person who attends a church on Easter or who sends his children to a church school or who calls a minister for a wedding or a funeral ought to bear an individual share of the load. But does he? No. The main load is carried by a third or less of the potential. Somehow it all reminds me of a remark by the late W. C. Fields. He came up in show business the hard way, and he had a healthy respect for money. When a casual acquaintance once asked for a loan, his answer was, "I'll see what my lawyer says—and if he says yes, I'll get another lawyer." Commendable as his reply might have been under the circumstances, there are all too many people who—in effect—are saying the same thing with respect to giving for the legitimate work of the Lord.

I began this chapter with the experience of a man in the rough-and-tumble world of politics. Let me close it with the experience of one in the hard-driving world of big-time auto racing. Roger Ward, who has won many races, including the Indianapolis 500, came out of World War II to learn auto racing the hard way on the small-time circuits, racing two or three times a week, risking his life on poor tracks and abused machinery with every lap. After one crash he couldn't drive for five months. The most common escape from the tensions of his profession was that old tranquilizer alcohol. Roger got quite a reputation; then he met a girl who soon meant the world to him. But for four years she said "No," and then, finally, when she did marry him, she often wished she hadn't. Roger was trying hard, however; he was moving upward; he was trying to lay off the booze; he was trying to make her happy. At her suggestion they began to tithe; they kept it up through thick and thin. He began to find it easier to pass up a drink, and one New Year's he poured a drink that had been handed him over a porch railing. "That," he said, "is that." And it was. And later, after he won at Indianapolis, when a reporter asked him if winning that race was his greatest victory, he said it wasn't. The thing that meant more to him than winning the 500 was to know that he had conquered himself. That is a victory every one of us needs, sooner or later, in one way or another! And, by the grace of God, it may come to us as it did to him—when we begin to discipline ourselves by putting 10 percent or more of our income into the best of all investments.

Mind the Light!

I read not long ago that the Coast Guard has success-
fully developed some sort of automatic, nuclear-
powered buoy light which will go for a year or more
without human attention of any sort. I am sure it will
help to establish a greater margin of safety for "those
who go down to the sea in ships," and I rejoice in that.
I know that it represents progress, and progress is a most
important product. It is a small example of automation,
and I am sure that automation is here to stay. But, even
as I read approvingly, I couldn't help thinking that it
must also represent the death knell of lighthouses and
all the romantic and heroic lore which has grown up
around them. I would think that anyone who had ever
taken a youngster to visit one of the nation's few re-
maining lighthouses would find it a little sad to think
that future generations of boys and girls won't have
such awe-inspiring and imagination-stirring places
to visit. And, preachers' minds being what they are, it
also reminded me of a true story from an earlier generation.

Mrs. Jacob Walker was taken as a bride to the Sandy
Hook lighthouse. She liked it there, for it was on a point

of the mainland, and she could keep a garden for vegetables and flowers. But after a few years her husband was transferred to Robbins Reef. When they got there, she said she wouldn't stay. "Water, water everywhere" made her lonely and blue. At first she refused even to unpack her trunks and boxes, but gradually she did. One night, while tending the light, her husband caught cold. It turned into pneumonia, and he had to be taken to Staten Island for hospitalization, but she could not leave the light even to be with him. A few days later they brought her the news that he had died. She once told a reporter: "We buried him in the cemetery on the hill. Every morning when the sun comes up I stand at the porthole and look in the direction of his grave. Sometimes the hills are white with snow. Sometimes they are green. Sometimes brown. But there always seems to come a message from that grave. It is what I heard Jacob say more often than anything else in his life. Just three words: 'Mind the light.'" When she told that to her interviewer, she was seventy years old; her husband had been dead for thirty-two years, and she was still minding the light.

It seems to me that there is a parable of the church here. Jesus said, "I am the light of the world" (John 8:12). And "mind the light!" is about as good a three-word summary of his last words to his disciples, variously reported as they are, as one is likely to find. We believe that the church's purpose is to continue and to expand Jesus' work in the world—it is its job to mind the light.

I

The church is called to mind the light of human decency. In Morris West's novel *The Ambassador,* which revolves around intrigue, treachery, corruption, power politics and double-dealing in a situation like Vietnam, there is a striking comment made by an embassy aide: "Somewhere, sometime, in all this bloody tangle of politics and diplomacy, a simple human decency has to enter. Someone has to affirm that a Chinese has as much right to eat as a Californian . . . and that the world can't be run by policemen and intelligence agents."

This is a needed word for our time. "Somewhere, sometime, in all this bloody tangle . . . a simple human decency has to enter." When one looks at the sleazy "realism" which seems to characterize so many of the books being published today, one wants to say: somewhere a simple human decency has to enter. When one reads of night rider killings and of juries which regard Negroes or civil rights workers as something less than human, one wants to say: somewhere a simple human decency has to enter.

When the cribbing scandals broke at the Air Force Academy, a friend of mine picked up a newspaper with an article discussing why young people get involved in this kind of trouble. The journalist pointed out that when a youngster is six years old, he sees his father slip a traffic officer five dollars to forget a speeding citation. When he is eight years old, he hears his mother and father discussing ways to cut corners on their income tax, explaining that "everybody does it." When he is twelve, he breaks his glasses and hears his mother tell the insurance company that they were stolen, thus collecting the price of a new pair. When he's out for the high school football team, the coach shows him how to catch hold of his opponent's shirt while blocking, or swivel a surreptitious hip into a pass receiver. When he gets his first job in a supermarket, he learns how to put the firm tomatoes on the top of the box, with the over-ripe ones underneath, or how to sell the same broom over and over again at the check-out stand. Maybe that same year his older brother, who is six feet tall and still growing, gets twenty offers from colleges that would like to have him play basketball, finally deciding on the one which gives him "the full ride" plus a convertible and a scholarship for his girl friend. Maybe he himself gets into a service academy although he's only a marginal student, while a friend of his in the top 3 percent of the class is rejected because he doesn't play football. Then an upperclassman sells him some exam answers for three dollars; he is caught in a cheating scandal and washed-out. Meanwhile the commandant is passing out press releases about cleaning out the bad apples from the barrel, and his folks wonder how he could ever have done a thing like that! The newspaperman adds with heavy sarcasm, "If there is one thing the adult world can't stand, it's a kid who cheats."

I have the feeling that the greatest threat to our way of life is not communism, dangerous as that is; and it is not the John Birchers or the hippies or the antiwar demonstrators. It is the easy and casual compromises we are all making with simple human decency. If the church doesn't mind that light, who will?

II

The church is called to mind the light of personal involvement. How often we all find ourselves saying, or thinking, "I don't want to get involved." One of the great perils of the computer age is that it makes noninvolvement easier. We cannot only "let George do it"; now we can also let the computer do it! And even worse, the vast capacities and amazing speeds of the computers, the experts are telling us, will make further centralization and overall planning necessary. Even now we are finding that to argue with a Secretary of Defense, for example, a man must have done an equal amount of computer homework—and there are only a few places in the country where such homework could be done! The flame of personal involvement and individual responsibility is bound to flicker low under such circumstances.

The current of history seems to alternate between the poles of the one and the many, the individual and the group. You can see this in the Bible. For a time in ancient Israel the current was flowing strongly toward the group; everyone thought and acted in terms of the nation as a whole. Then with Jeremiah and Ezekiel it began to flow the other way—toward the importance of the individual and his personal responsibility. Both quote a popular proverb, "The fathers have eaten sour grapes, and the children's teeth are set on edge"—that is, we are punished individually for the sins of humanity —and refuted it, "Every one shall die for his own sin; each man who eats sour grapes, his teeth shall be set on edge" (Jer. 31:29-30; see also Ezek. 18:2-4). But with the Second Isaiah and Ezra's codification of the Law the current began to flow the other way again.

You can see this in the alternation from autocratic kings to Greek democracy back to the Roman Empire. You can see it in the history of the church itself; it began with many almost isolated centers and moved toward a unity which reached its climax in the famous medieval synthesis of the thirteenth century when all the institutions of Western civilization—domestic, political, educational, economic—centered in the church. Then the Renaissance and Reformation started the current going the other way. All the great revolutions from 1500 to 1900 were movements away from unity toward diversity. And now the tide has turned again; the predominant flow of our time is toward unity, authority, and control.

We are not likely to change the pattern, and it is probable that in ways we do not even now foresee, history's current will again turn toward the individual. But in the meantime there are values and freedoms too precious to be allowed to perish, even though they may be muted. And since it is often the duty of the church to "strengthen the opposite of that which is too strong," it is one of the church's functions in our time to mind the light of personal responsibility and individual involvement.

Comedian Dick Gregory tells about an incident from his boyhood that still burns brightly in his memory. He had had a good day selling papers and shining shoes, and he went into a restaurant and got a veritable feast—a bowl of chili, a cheeseburger, a soft drink, and a piece of chocolate cake. As he ate, an old wino came in, ordered twenty-six cents worth of food, and made the most of every bite. When it was time to pay the check, he simply said he didn't have any money, whereupon the owner knocked him down with a bottle, watched him bleed a little, and then began to kick him. Then young Dick Gregory said, "Leave him alone; I'll pay the twenty-six cents." The wino managed to pull himself up, and then leaning on the counter, said, "Keep your twenty-six cents. You don't have to pay, not now. I just finished paying for it." He started out; then he put his hand on the boy's shoulder and with the venom in his voice replaced by sadness, said, "Thanks, Sonny, but it's too late now. Why didn't you pay it before?" Young Gregory realized that he had waited too long to help another man. He had avoided getting involved; he had shrugged something off as not his responsibility. He had done the same thing thirty-eight people did in New York as a girl was being manhandled and murdered; he had done the same thing the concentration camp guards and minor bureaucrats in Hitler's Germany had done. If the church doesn't mind the light of personal involvement, who will?

There is a Spanish proverb which goes, " 'Take what you want,' says God, 'and pay for it.' " As with most proverbs it does not cover the whole of experience, but it is a capsule comment embodying a good deal of practical wisdom. The truth of it is illustrated by an incident in the Old Testament. Abram and Lot had come a long way and gone through much together; fortune had smiled on them and they were well-off patriarchal heads of large establishments, "rich in cattle, in silver, and in gold." Most of their wealth was in the form of livestock, and their herds became so great that "the land could not support both of them dwelling together"—there wasn't enough range or enough water, and their hired hands fell to fighting and quarreling over who should have what. So they decided to part, and Abram gave his nephew the first choice. "So Lot chose for himself all the Jordan valley, and . . . Abram dwelt in the land of Canaan" (Gen. 13). Henceforth, having made their choices, they had to live with them and pay for them, even as do you and I. Life seems to be organized rather like a supermarket—you take what you want and pay for it.

When we get involved, we learn that *there are problems in the use and handling of material possessions.* The cause of Abram and Lot's separation was their property. Property so often is a source of friction! One of the things that drove a wider and wider wedge between the North and the South in the days before the Civil War was the question of whether a slave was a human being or a piece of property. In the end, economic historians tell us, we spent more than twice as much to fight the war as it would have cost to buy every slave in the land in 1860! Since time began, I suppose, property, wealth, material possessions, have been a cause of strife. They cause domestic discord; they raise problems of national policy; families have been split by them; friends have become bitter enemies over them.

An Oklahoma publication once sponsored a contest for the best essay suggested by two pictures, one of a dilapidated house and the other of a badly eroded field. The first prize went to a Cherokee Indian who wrote:

Both pictures show white man crazy. Make big tepee. Plow hill. Water wash. Wind blow soil. Grass all gone. Squaw gone, papoose too. No chuckaway. No pig, no corn, no hay, no cow, no pony. Indian no plow land. Keep grass. Buffalo eat. Indian eat buffalo. Hide make tepee, moccasins, too. Indian no make terrace. No build dam. No give a damn. All time eat. No hunt job. No hitchhike. No ask relief. Great Spirit make grass. Indian no waste anything. White man much crazy.

It sounds reasonable! And yet, the Indians had not really solved the problem of the use of property. Under their hand this continent supported only a fraction of the people it does now. They only made a minimum use of what God put here.

Some have thought of poverty as the answer. Emmett McLoughlin, a former Roman Catholic priest, has told about an experience he had as a young Franciscan monk. (The Franciscans, you know, take vows of poverty.) At the end of each meal toothpicks were passed. Some of the young monks noticed that they seemed soiled and frayed so they secretly marked a few. Sure enough, they turned up at the next meal for use again. One of the brothers was salvaging them from the garbage! "Even the Superior admitted that neither St. Francis nor the Pope wanted poverty carried that far."

If minimum use and voluntary poverty do not solve the problem of property, does maximum production and prosperity take care of it? No. There has not been a notable increase in domestic harmony or national righteousness in these recent years. According to a study made by the American Institute of Public Opinion, most of us are dissatisfied with what we have. "Seven out of every ten adults feel that more money would contribute substantially to their happiness. The average of how much more a week they figure it would take is thirty-seven dollars." The more you have, the more you want!

Once more, the story of Abram and Lot teaches us that *the result of magnanimity is the extension of personality and influence.* The story exalts the ideal qualities of Abram's character: peaceful, generous, humble. At its close he is pictured as receiving the ideal reward: a promise from God that his posterity will be a great people—his personality and influence were to be infinitely extended.

The story is as true to life as it can be. The result of minding the light by just and generous dealing is the extension of your personality and influence. There was once a man who made a fortune in real estate. But an economic "panic" pricked his bubble, leaving him land-poor, $100,000 in debt, and with his home mortgaged to the hilt. In his discouragement he began to study the Bible, and the great truth of generous living dawned upon him. He promised himself that from then on he was going to be generous in his giving for the work of the Lord.

He became interested in a small soap and drug business. Out of it he developed a product which he called Mentholatum. The business began to grow. He gave 10 percent of his income; he got his debts paid, and the business grew still more so he began to give more—20, 30, 40, 50, and finally 90 percent—of his income. His name was A. A. Hyde. John R. Mott, the beloved ecumenical leader, once said that he could not name a single nation—and he had traveled all over the world—where he had not personally seen the great influences which had come from the life of A. A. Hyde. The astute journalist William Allen White wrote: "This man is rich but beloved, not for what he has earned but for what he has given away."

The result of involvement is the extension of your personality and influence.

It is not often that one sees any very obvious results from church school or morning worship. Yet every now and then I get a letter which assures me that the game is more than worth the candle. Let me share one or two with you.

The first one is part of one received from some people who had fallen on evil days and had been encouraged by one or two little things I had been able to do:

We admit the going has been tough for a few months, but we have had bad breaks before and by clinging to our faith in a just God have come out on top. This time we have reason to feel very humble, for friends have been exceptionally kind. We wonder if we are deserving of so much. Our years of Christian service in the church were the best years of our lives. . . . If we were able to help the church in its great task, we are glad.

The other letter came from a family in the first church I ever served, a family whom I was fortunate enough to unite in their loyalty to the church. One summer the husband, although hardly fifty years old, suffered a heart attack. He was recovering nicely and was about to return to work when he suffered another one. His wife wrote to me:

He will never work again . . . if he continues to follow this pattern the outlook is for another attack shortly. . . . They expect one from four to six months. . . . Now do you realize how wonderful it is we were both in church? We felt we wasted so many years. . . . This is Audrey's last year in high school; she wants to go to the university and take religious education but will have to do it entirely on her own. I had hoped originally to help her with her fees and carfare but now it is impossible. . . . Best wishes in your church. Just give them half of what we got and . . . sometime they'll draw help.

Our late ambassador to the United Nations, Adlai Stevenson, used to tell about a preacher who had so moved one of his hearers that the latter jumped to his feet and said, "O Lord, use me. Use me, O Lord—in an advisory capacity!" There is a ready supply of that kind of dedication! God and his church do not need more advisors as much as more of those who will give practical and effective support by their prayers, their attendance, their gifts, and their service. The call is for each of us to help the church mind the lights of human decency and personal involvement.

The Worst Kind of Heart Trouble

Fred Allen, the late radio comedian extraordinary, started in show business in vaudeville. In his autobiography he tells about the big-time houses and circuits of the roaring twenties. As the decade began to wane, two rivals began to climb: moving pictures and radio. But, he comments, "the vaudeville-circuit heads had their money stacked so high they couldn't look over it to see what was happening to the big-time." And, of course, as we look back now, we can see that it wasn't very long before vaudeville was dead.

Jesus once told a story about a man who made a similar mistake (Luke 12:16-21). He was a man who had it made; his money was stacked so high he couldn't see over it; he was sitting pretty. "But God said to him, 'Fool! This night your soul is required of you; and the things you have prepared, whose will they be?' " That is just about as scornfully cutting a remark as Jesus ever made. The English translation is far weaker than the original, which breathes the spirit of strong language born of exasperation. Its force is more like this: "But God said to him, 'You damned fool. . . .' "

Personally, there are a lot of things I would rather be called than that! In fact, I would rather be called almost anything else than that. The Gospels record only one other time when Jesus mentioned such an epithet, and there he ranks its use as serious enough to jeopardize one's eternal destiny (Matt. 5:22). So he must have had strong reasons for using so strong an expression. Was it scorn for the rich? There is no reason to think so; Jesus never condemned anyone for making or having money. He knew as well as anyone that we can't live without money and the things it can buy. His group had its treasurer (John 13:29). He once used the wise investment of money as a parable (Matt. 25:14-30), and he saw in one shrewd operator a lesson in prudence (Luke 16:1-8). The story in Luke about the rich man who built bigger barns doesn't intimate that the man was dishonest or ruthless; he was not mean or miserly; he expected to eat, drink, and be merry, and that hardly sounds like a scrooge.

Still, Jesus regarded this eminently successful man as a fool. *He called him a fool because he made a foolish use of what he had.* He was doing the same thing, in a different way, as the people Haggai describes as putting their money into "a bag with holes" (1:1-9). He wasn't getting full value out of it; he wasn't getting big enough or permanent enough returns on it; he stood to lose it all. He had it stacked up so high he couldn't see anyone else; he was all wrapped up in himself. His little soliloquy is composed of forty-six words (in Greek), and more than a fourth of them (twelve) are "I" or "my" or their equivalents: "*I* will do this," "*My* grain . . . *my* goods . . . *my* barns." He never gave a thought to anything beyond his own private affairs and his personal pleasure. As Bob Hope put it, "If you haven't got charity in your heart, you have the worst kind of heart trouble."

I

The only way to avoid that kind of heart trouble is to get all wrapped up in others. Jesus held that the least act of kindness done to a human being was done personally to him, and that the smallest cruelty done to a human being was done to him.

I once was a judge in a poster-making contest. The posters were for the promotion of a missionary fund. One of those posters sticks in my mind yet. It was in the form of a mobile, hanging by a thread from the ceiling. The cross arm was made out of an old coat hanger, tipped lower at one end than the other like the beam of a scale. At the low end there hung a cardboard world with pictures on it of some of the earth's needy peoples. And on the other end hung two words, "Mission Fund." The phrase on the crossbar was this: "It hardly balances."

How often that is true! How often our thoughts and prayers and efforts and gifts hardly balance the need! We are hardly balancing our needs for schools these days; we are hardly balancing our need for teachers and doctors; we are hardly balancing the need for clean air and pure water and peace among men. The only way I see to avoid the worst kind of heart trouble in times like these is to get all wrapped up in others' hopes and needs.

I once had the opportunity to do a kindness for a person from out of state. The thank-you note was far from routine, and the last line was the best of all: "And, as I found long ago, I may have little opportunity to do the same for you, but I pay my 'debt' by standing ready to open my heart to some other person—this is the way it was meant to be. My God is a positive one, and I do my best when I stay on the plus side." That's it! No heart trouble there! The only way to avoid it is to get all wrapped up in others.

II

Secondly, *Jesus calls for* what I would call *intelligent extravagance.* Although that sounds like a contradiction in terms, I am convinced that there is such a thing. It means spending or giving or doing something more than the minimum or the necessary. It is giving "good measure, pressed down, shaken together" (Luke 6:38) ; it is the kind of thing Jesus commended in the woman with the ointment (Mark 14:3-9) . It is intelligent extravagance to buy something a little more than you can afford for someone you really love. It is intelligent extravagance to take time, even though you are busy and tired, to do something with your children.

A bishop who was in Istanbul a few years ago was the guest of a Father Demetrius of the Orthodox Church. Father Demetrius took the bishop and his wife to a bazaar to make some last-minute purchases. They were entertained with typical Near Eastern courtesy before the trading began, and as they sipped their tea, the business man said to the bishop: "You are with a good man. He thinks everybody is good, and I am not even tempted to cheat anyone when he is here." A little later the Orthodox priest bought a ring. After he had paid for it, the shopkeeper told the bishop that Father Demetrius could not afford the ring, but he was buying it for a girl whose parents had lost their home and business in some recent rioting. Father Demetrius overheard the remark, and half-shamefacedly admitted as much. "I suppose," he said, "I ought to give her some shoes or a coat, but I did not want to give a gift to remind her of her poverty. I want her to know that she is loved."

That is intelligent extravagance! That is the kind of giving that prevents the worst kind of heart trouble! And it is for such a spirit in our living and our giving that Jesus called for.

There is a very clear and fine note in that incident from the life of David which is recorded in II Sam. 24: 18-25. Events had sobered David and turned his thoughts Godward. He determined on an act of religious devotion, and there being yet no central and official place of worship in Israel, he decided to build an altar on which to lay his offerings. The ideal spot was a threshing floor owned by a man named Araunah, and David went to talk to him about it. Araunah was impressed and honored that the king would come wanting to buy something from him. (It is a little as though the President's wife should stop by your house someday and see an antique chair which she wanted for the White House and ask you how much you wanted for it. You might well say to her that you wouldn't sell it, but that you would be honored to give it the White House.) So Araunah offered to give the king the threshing floor and as many animals as he wanted for his ceremony and the wood for the fire that would be required. Then comes the great line: "But the king said to Araunah, 'No, but I will buy it of you for a price; I will not offer burnt offerings to the Lord my God which cost me nothing.'" That is about as good a one-sentence summary of the biblical view of giving as can be found. Our gifts must not be those which cost little or nothing; they are to be the very best that we can give. An altar and a burnt offering may reflect a rather primitive kind of religion, but no one whose religion really costs him nothing has a right to dismiss David's attitude. He was on the right track; no religious devotion is worthy of the name which does not cost the giver something real, something substantial, something sacrificial.

Do you remember how Jesus commended the poor widow who threw a couple of coppers in the temple offering? The thing he noted about it was that it was all she had. It would have been easy for her to rationalize herself into giving only half of it and using the rest to buy bread. She could have gone further and thought that she not only needed to eat, but that she had a responsibility for the education of her children, or this, or that, or a thousand other things. Her gift was a great one because it was sacrificial; it wasn't something she could easily spare, or by careful management do as well without; it was something that meant doing without for herself and her family.

I saw a modern parallel to that woman a few years ago. A visitor had spoken to a small group in a private home about stewardship. Not only was his logic good, his spirit was infectious, and after the discussion which followed I heard a graduate student's wife say, with a hint of a sigh, "There goes our new rug." I happened to know that she had been scrimping and saving for that rug; although she had children of her own she had been earning a little extra by taking care of others' in order to get enough for it. But she decided that day to give it to the church. I can only say that she gave me a new insight into what God expects of us all.

A missionary was leaving his field of service to return to his own country. He had been there a long time and was widely respected and loved by those whom he had tried to serve. They gave him a farewell party, and each one attending brought a gift. Finally, after the others had given their gifts and gone, one shyly brought him a seashell. As the missionary looked at it, he saw not only the carefully cleaned and polished shell but the long journey to the coast and back which it had meant. He commented on it appreciatively, and the other replied with a smile, "Long walk part of gift." When you come down to it, that is what the Bible means by giving that is liberal, faithful, sacrificial—it means giving that involves one's whole self. "Long walk part of gift."

82

I believe with all my heart, therefore, that tithing is good preventive medicine; it can save you from the worst kind of heart trouble. The giving of 10 percent or more of your income inevitably tends to get you wrapped up in others, "for where your treasure is, there will your heart be also" (Luke 12:34). It makes possible that kind of intelligent extravagance which lets people know that they are loved rather than reminding them of their poverty. I have never known anyone who, having once started tithing, ever found any system more satisfying.

A Christian farmer in Brazil had sold his year's crop and had immediately put a tenth of the receipts, about $110, into his pocket and started for the church to give it to the pastor. It was some distance to town; the day was hot; the road was dusty as he walked along. He had gone only about halfway when his oldest son came running after him, calling for him to come home right away. A forest fire had already reached the other side of their farm! He got home in time to see only the smoldering ruins of his house; the fire, driven by a brisk wind, had taken hold so fast that chickens had been roasted as they sat hatching eggs. Even the family dog had been caught in the holocaust.

There was nothing to do but to try to find a place for the family to stay; he appointed one of his boys to do that and said he was going to town to give his tithe to the church. His family couldn't understand it; that $110 was all they had in the world; his oldest son argued all the way to town with him. The farmer never mentioned his loss to his pastor; he just said that this was his annual tithe and that he was grateful for what the Lord had done for him. The oldest son later told the minister what had happened. The minister had an emergency meeting of his church officials within hours. A relatively new Christian in the group was so impressed by the farmer's fidelity he promised to give half of all he had to help him and the others who had been burned out, and his gift amounted to $12,000. By nightfall a committee from the church had found the farmer and told him that they had deposited $610 in a special bank account to help him get a new start.

The moral of the story for me is not that if you're a tither things will always work out in the best way for you. Sometimes they do; sometimes they don't. It is not my experience that tithing brings any special favors your way. The thing that impressed me raises a question I would like you to put to yourself. Is your giving the kind that would inspire others? Would other people in your church, if they knew how much you were giving, be inspired to do more, or would your giving justify their doing less? If your pledges are the kind that would inspire others to give more, it can be safely said that you will never suffer from the worst kind of heart trouble!

Questions Everyone Asks

Whenever the spending of money comes up as a topic for discussion, there are at least a few questions that everyone asks. And in a church the question of spending money comes up with every new budget or every building fund campaign! So let us give some thought to these proper and recurring questions.

Christian stewardship is more than a response to emotional appeals or emergency situations. There is an old story about a man who went to church when some sort of special effort was under way. When the offering plate was passed, he put in a bill. Then, surprisingly, a little later another offering was taken; he contributed some halves and quarters. What to his wondering eye should appear still later but another offering; he dropped in the rest of his change. As the ushers began to start down the aisle for the fourth time, a sweet little old lady sitting next to him, evidently a visitor, leaned over and put into words the question that was forming in his own mind: "What do they do now, search us?"

In taking up these questions I have no desire or intention of trying to embarrass anyone. Giving in the church is and ought to be wholly and completely voluntary and individual. I simply want to try to give some honest answers to these well-nigh universal questions.

I

Several questions invariably come up whenever money is to be spent. The first question is usually: *How much does it cost?* In the case of a church the answer is whatever the total budget or goal may be. And that, in turn, is to most, quite a sizable amount of money. Is it an arbitrary figure, one plucked from the sky? Or is it an honest and realistic one? Church budgets and building costs are given careful consideration; experts are consulted, and much planning takes place before a final figure is submitted to the congregation. The figure may often be large, but it is an honest assessment.

The second question that is likely to come up when money is to be spent is this: *Have we got the money?* Can we afford it? In our personal affairs most of us have to think twice about that, and it is always a proper consideration in the church, too. Tony Cuccinello made an interesting comment when the pennant races were coming down to the wire one year. Tony was a coach for the Chicago White Sox; he was also the uncle of Sam Mele, who was managing the league-leading Minnesota Twins. Someone asked him if he was pulling for Sam, and he replied: "When Sam's playing the Yankees or the Orioles, I root for him, naturally. But when it comes down to the big thing," that is, when the Twins were playing the White Sox, "you know how I'm rooting. Money is thicker than blood." Money is thicker than a lot of

things for most of us, and the question is whether or not
we think we have enough for a particular expenditure.

Few, if any, of us feel as though we've got any extra
money. We know that the cost of living has been going
up more or less steadily for twenty-five years. Some of
us may have a kindred feeling for that fellow who heard
about the war on poverty and wanted to know where
he could go to surrender!

At the same time, we are in a period of almost un-
paralleled prosperity. Wages and profits are high; unem-
ployment is low. The newspaper reports that the effective buying power of families increased 43 percent in
ten years! The average family now spends a smaller
percentage of a larger income on the basic necessities
than it used to. The nation's per capita income from
wages, dividends, and pensions jumped 6 percent in one
year alone. Corporate profits are up. An average offering
of three dollars a week, or more, from each family is
possible for most of us when there is a building fund
drive. Of course, a few people cannot give as much as
that, and some will not give as little as that, but there
can hardly be any reasonable doubt that we have the
money.

The third question which invariably comes up, in the
thrifty shopper's mind at any rate, is this: *Could we get
the same thing cheaper somewhere else?* Most of us like
to get a bargain, if we can, and none of us like to be
taken in by fast talk or glib promises and end up spending more than necessary.

Can we get what we want cheaper? It would, of

course, be possible to build a less adequate building, but it would not do what we had wanted it to do, its appearance and durability would suffer, and there would be less space available. Again, I am sure that we could attend churches which didn't require large buildings, but in that case there would be fewer people to share the load, and the cost per family might well be higher.

Taking the question in a larger context, we might wonder whether we could not get our religion, so to speak, cheaper somewhere else. I am ashamed to say that I hardly know where one would go to get religion as cheaply as we do in our churches! That is true of us as a generation. With national income at all-time high levels we're actually giving a smaller proportion for all philanthropic and benevolent causes than our fathers did a generation ago! That is true of us as Christians. A Muslim is required to give 2½ percent—not of his income, but of his total wealth—annually; and Whittaker Chambers tells us that Communists give 10 percent of their incomes to the Party. Could we get by cheaper somewhere else? I suppose so, but I am ashamed to say that I hardly know where.

II

But the most important question of all to be answered when money is to be spent is this: *Will the purchase give satisfaction?* Will it be a good buy in the long run? Will I be glad I got it, or wish I hadn't? Will it be so much money wasted, or money well spent?

That is the crucial question because it is the question

we are all asking about life. Someone wrote a letter not long ago the final paragraph of which read as follows: "Perhaps you wouldn't mind sending me some advice as to just what to do to be able to lead a fuller, richer and successful life in these trying days." Most of us could have written those lines, could we not? Most of us are interested in leading fuller, richer, more successful lives than we are. All of us, at times, feel that life has somehow passed us by, that we've lived more or less on the margins and on the fringes, that there is considerably more richness and depth and satisfaction in life than we seem to be getting out of it.

There is a line in scripture which speaks to our condition. "So he built an altar there and called upon the name of the Lord, and pitched his tent there. And . . . dug a well" (Gen. 26:25). Nothing extraordinary there; in fact, pretty ordinary for an ancient Hebrew. He was centering his life on three things—his work (the well was to provide water for his flocks) ; his home, for he was a nomad and lived all his life in tents; and his worship. It may be a trinity worth thinking about a little further when we are asking ourselves how to get the most for our money and for our lives.

Let us look first at our daily work. One of the greatest sources of personal satisfaction is to have given one's best to some sort of socially useful and constructive work.

In one of Rembrandt's etchings now in the Metropolitan Museum of Art in New York City, Jesus is portrayed in the act of driving the money changers out of the temple. The most curious thing about this particular work of the artist is that there is no halo around the head of the Galilean; instead there is one around the hand which holds the scourge. The usual explanation of art experts is that Rembrandt was a Protestant and unfamiliar with the proper use of halos. Whether that is true or not, the thought is suggestive. A halo around the hand! Has not God put a halo around every hand? Does he not wish to sanctify the work of our hands? Isn't it part of his great design that work should have a sacred meaning and purpose? He certainly put plenty of it here for the sons of men to do!

One of the great unsolved problems facing our American way of life is our attitude toward work. The prevalent idea seems to be that work is a curse. It is something to be avoided wherever and whenever possible. There is a notion that if you're really smart you won't have to work. Many are looking for a shortcut to success. You can see this failure in the construction worker leaning on his shovel over a cigarette and in the secretary whose break for coffee gets longer and longer. You can see this failure in the unions which have encouraged "featherbedding"—forcing the employment of men who actually do no useful work—and in the industries that have so simplified a man's part in production that it is next to impossible for him to have any sense of creativity at all. For a great many people the ideal society would be one where everyone could take it easy. "Shorter hours, plenty to eat, nothing to worry about, the comforts of life—isn't that what is meant by hosts of people when they think about the kind of a world we ought to have?"

On the contrary! Work is one of God's greatest blessings for his children. He has made us co-workers with him. An unorthodox but true definition of a gentleman, I believe, is that he "is one who does not live on the sweat of someone else's brow." The psychiatrists and heart specialists are telling us these days that far greater dangers attend underwork than overwork.

> My Master was a worker,
> With daily work to do,
> And he who would be like Him
> Must be a worker too.
> Then welcome honest labor,
> And honest labor's fare.
> For where there is a worker
> The Master's man is there.

Another thing that the verse from Genesis suggests for those who want to live more abundant lives is the sharing of a home. Isaac pitched a tent. It would be difficult to name a potential source of more abiding satisfaction than participation in a Christian home.

Yet it is no secret that many aren't finding happiness at home. One of the bad moments in the life of King David occurred on the day he came home bringing the Ark of the Lord to Jerusalem after a hard campaign. In the manner of the time and in the frenzy of victorious joy he danced before the Ark in celebration. Then he ordered a sacrifice and a public feast. When it was all over, he headed for home where, unbeknown to him, his wife Michal had been watching from the window. She hadn't liked what she had seen. It had seemed indecent and unworthy to her, and the writer says that she "despised him in her heart." Her first words were heavy with sarcasm, "How the king of Israel honored himself today!" That was ominous. When your wife uses your official title, you may know that a storm is brewing! She proceeded, in a few well-selected words, to give him a piece of her mind. David, taken by surprise and a man of some spunk himself, flared back at her to the effect that he didn't care what she thought—there were other women who hadn't thought he had done so badly! And one thing led to another until a day which had started out in rejoicing ended in a bitter quarrel (II Sam. 6:16-23). Not much joy and satisfaction there!

Look at this matter of the home in another way. My heart is heavy and I think God's heart is heavy for the homes in our land. The Christian faith tells us that we all really belong to one home; we are all one family. Yet we read of people burning crosses on the lawns of others' homes and still say, "We have no problems of racial prejudice." We fight abroad for freedom, yet we restrict freedom here because we are afraid we might lower the property values! Of course, it is not true that the moving of nonwhites into a white neighborhood lowers values—as scientific sociological studies have shown. But supposing it were true! Can we as Christians put property above personality? Could we who stand for, and gain so much from, the family and the home deny equal opportunities to others?

Another thing the verse from Genesis suggests as the way to abundant living is an altar. Isaac built an altar —a place of worship. He gave religion its rightful place in his life.

There is a short story told in the seventy-third psalm. It is the story of a man who went to church depressed. The experiences of life were eating away at his faith. He was getting cynical. He looked around, and he saw arrogance prospering; the crooks seemed to be the only ones making any money; the injustice of the world was making him bitter. Clearly, he wasn't enjoying life much. Then he went to church. And he came out a different man. His faith was restored; his ideals were polished; his morale was lifted. Envy and jealousy were gone, and so were his doubts. He felt at peace with the world and glad to be alive. It had all seemed a "wearisome task" to him until he "went into the sanctuary of God." Worship made the difference.

He is not the only man who has found it so. It has been the experience of mankind through the ages. More psychologists are discovering every day that there is healing and health-giving power in worship.

Bishop Earl Ledden, in a message which dealt with the industrial strife, the political corruption, and the international tensions which beset us, held up Christ as the answer. He concluded by quoting a line of a hymn, "There's no other way but His way," and remarked that he couldn't remember at the moment just what hymn it was from. The mail he got seemed to reveal that everyone but he knew where it came from! He got songbooks, pages torn from hymnals, typewritten and handwritten copies of the old revival favorite:

What do you hope, dear brother,
To gain by a further delay?
There's no one to save you but Jesus,
There's no other way but His way.

At first the bishop was chagrined; he thought he had missed the boat in relating our complex social problems to the mass hypnosis of the sawdust trail. But then the deeper truth began to dawn on him. The longer he reflected the plainer it became that "what this generation needs above all else is an altar call." The form and method must vary from generation to generation as it always has, but the fundamental fact holds that "this world is doomed and damned apart from God. It is not enough to seek political solutions or economic salvation." We need a people seriously intent upon the religious life.

Will a new building be a good investment in the long run? It will if it pays regular dividends in church life. It will if it pays long-term dividends with youth. It will if it pays dividends for the neighborhood (one of the reasons the church's service to its neighborhood is often spotty is that it often has poor ways, at best, of providing what the neighborhood needs most). And it will if it pays lasting dividends in personal satisfaction to all who have had a part in making it possible. To build it is to dig a well, pitch a tent, and raise an altar!

One of the wartime speeches of Winston Churchill was a brief address to the House of Commons outlining his administration's policy about rebuilding the Houses of Parliament which had been bombed and gutted by fire. When the time came, they were going to rebuild the Commons just like it had been before; they were not going to modernize it or make it more functional. Their reason was not mere sentiment. It was because of the strength which the continuing tradition of the "mother of parliaments" represented, a tradition symbolized, if anywhere, in the very brick and mortar and paneling and shape and size of that building. Twenty years later there was a sequel to that speech. Churchill had announced that he would not be a candidate in the fall elections. When he rose to leave the House for what everyone knew was the last time, "the old bulldog turned at the door and faced the chair. The bow was nearly imperceptible, but it was there." Then he went out, and the massive doors closed on the man who not merely rebuilt the Commons, but had rallied his fellows to share in England's finest hour. There are few things which bring to human hearts as much satisfaction as having shared in some way in something greater than themselves!

Let me close this chapter with a word about a passage from the Gospels (Mark 3:1-6). It is a strange passage to think of in connection with building fund campaigns. It says nothing about giving or pledging money.

It is the account of the incident in the life of Jesus which is usually referred to as "the man with the withered hand." Some of Jesus' critics were there and were covertly looking for some misstep on his part, and he knew it. Then Mark says a word so bold and shocking that the other Gospel writers left it out: Jesus "looked around at them with anger, grieved at their hardness of heart" (3:5). The story is not only about the need of a man with a withered hand, but also about some good religious people with withered hearts. That is almost always a danger, and that is a test which comes to everyone —whether we will grieve our Lord by the hardness of our hearts, or grow more like him by our willingness to sacrifice for that which will heal and bless human life.

What Every Human Needs

Early in his career Charlie Chaplin was playing with a small vaudeville troupe; after five months of playing the sticks they had a week between engagements. He was one of the better paid members of the troupe, single, and without obligations, so he had been able to save quite a bit. He decided to refresh his jaded spirit by indulging himself in a few days of gracious living. He bought some expensive clothes and luggage, headed for New York, and took a room at the Hotel Astor. For a while he reveled in the deference offered him by bell-boys and waiters, in the gilt and plush of the lobby, in the sheer luxury of a private bath with hot and cold water. He dressed for dinner; in his best English accent he ordered consommé, roast chicken, and ice cream. He left the waiter a generous tip and strolled grandly to the opera. On his way back to the hotel he ran into a friend he hadn't seen for several years and had the pleasure of observing the effect of his nonchalant remark that he was staying at the Astor. But he stayed only one day; the next day he was on the train back to Philadelphia and looking forward eagerly to rejoining the other members of the troupe.

What had happened? Why would a sophisticated and

independent young man of the world cut short such idyllic delights to hurry back to the cheap company of tenth-rate vaudeville performers? He did it because he was lonely, because he wanted companionship, because of a deep need inside himself for friendship.

That is a need that every last one of us has. We are gregarious by nature; we need others of our kind around. Some of us, of course, are more social and outgoing than others; some of us are more reserved and withdrawn; but all of us need association with others. We are born helplessly dependent upon others, and most of us die the same way. Shut a person up in solitary confinement and in an incredibly brief time his mental equilibrium begins to go; he becomes queer, eccentric, odd.

When our troops were fighting in Korea, a journalist hitched a ride with a sergeant. As the jeep bounced along, the fighting man asked, "Are you just over from the States?" The editor replied that he was. The soldier wanted to know what the people back home were thinking and saying about the war. At last the sergeant said, "You know, it's a funny thing about this business of morale. It's not what a lot of people think it is. It isn't beer, and it isn't USO shows. Morale is the feeling that somehow you are connected up with the folks back home, and that they are connected up with you." The hunger of the heart for fellowship, the feeling that somehow you are connected up with others, and they with you—that is what every human needs.

I

Life does not just automatically supply man's need for fellowship. In fact, a pretty good case can be made for the position that the modern world, in particular, tends to deny or thwart this hunger of our spirits. As the pace of life speeds up, life seems also to become less personal. I was talking the other day with a ten-year-old boy who had to stop and think before he could tell me how many brothers he had. His father has been twice divorced, and neither his own mother nor his step-mother, apparently, thought enough of the boy to want him to live with them. It is a psychological and sociological commonplace that a youngster needs the fellowship of a family—a mother, father, brothers and sisters—if he is to have the best chance to develop normally and completely. Yet life doesn't automatically assure us that we'll have it.

A youth rally once used an interesting gimmick to demonstrate what the impersonalism of modern life does to us. The youth were divided, as they came, by an arbitrary and mechanical numbering system, and before anyone had any real chance to become acquainted with anyone else, they were sent by number to a particular room and seated on particular chairs. In this way all those who came with friends were completely separated, no one was sitting near anyone he knew, no name tags or ice-breaking introductions or games were used. I drew the assignment of trying to lead a group of about forty in a discussion under those conditions! There was no discussion; in forty-five minutes I succeeded in getting only about half a dozen of them even to open their mouths to make the briefest kind of statements. (I have been wondering since if there is some way of applying this technique to teen-agers' telephone conversations!) Fortunately, I wasn't supposed to get much discussion or produce any answers; the idea was to make them *feel* what depersonalizing does to people. It reminded me of the story about the fellow who tried to call a friend. He used the right area code number and the right telephone number, and he knew the other's auto license, bank check, social security, and credit card numbers; but a recorded voice at the other end of the line said, "I'm sorry; we don't have any number by that name here." Life, modern life at any rate, does not just automatically supply our human need for fellowship.

II

One of the church's main jobs is to provide fellowship. Perhaps I ought to put that even more strongly—it is the church's job to *be* a fellowship. In the book of Acts we read about one of the great days in the early church; according to the account, Peter took in about three thousand members that day (2:41). Note what it was they were taken into: "And they devoted themselves to the apostles' teaching and fellowship, to the breaking of bread and the prayers" (2:42). The church has an educational job, teaching; the church has a job

100

to do in worship ("the breaking of bread" is most likely a reference to the early communion service) and prayer. And there it is, right alongside these other important functions; the church has a job to do in fellowship.

One of the simplest and best definitions of the church's purpose is to say that it is to continue the work of Jesus in this world. That necessarily includes fellowship. When Jesus returned to Nazareth after hearing John preach, he borrowed a phrase from Isaiah to define his own work: "The Spirit of the Lord is upon me," he said, "because he has . . . sent me to proclaim release to the captives, . . . to set at liberty those who are oppressed" (Luke 4:18). Jesus didn't liberate his people politically from the Roman oppressor, and he didn't mastermind any jailbreaks. What he did was to release people from the oppression and captivity of their own isolation; he set them free from their own personality quirks, from their crippling inhibitions and paralyzing frustrations. And it is our business as Christians to help people out of the drab and defeating prisons of their shyness, their loneliness, their fears, their prejudices, their inferiority and guilt complexes by a warm and friendly fellowship.

One of the purposes of the church is "the maintenance of Christian fellowship and discipline, the edification of believers." It took me a long time to realize what "edify" means. I had thought of it chiefly in terms of intellectual enlightenment, but it basically means to

101

erect an edifice—to build a building. The edification of believers means building them up in the Christian life, and the chief means of doing it is through disciplined Christian fellowship.

Christian fellowship is something more than just fellowship. There are, and there ought to be, opportunities within the life of the church for people to get together in small groups for good times together. But Christian fellowship does more than provide a peer group, a place to belong, a place to find full acceptance. That kind of fellowship can be had in a tavern or at a football game. (I hope that I do not sound even faintly superior; to our shame we must confess that much church fellowship has not been as real as that found in a bar or at a sporting event.) But what the church is trying to do, however faulty and spotty its execution, is to provide opportunities for creatively interacting, disciplined fellowship that not merely accepts a person but helps him to grow more fully mature. Such fellowship can operate on many levels—from playschool classes for four-year-olds to a student program, from groups of hundreds down to a group of two: a minister counseling with someone who wants help with a problem. Again, it is difficult to say to what degree, if any, the church succeeds. But one young married couple who moved away not long ago wrote back, "We'll always remember your help as the beginning of a happier life for us." There can never come a time when such disciplined fellowship will not be helpful to humanity.

III

Let me quickly suggest some of the ways a local church fulfills this need for fellowship, which the world so often thwarts for so many.

It is obvious that a church's fellowship hall is designed to increase and enhance fellowship. In all seriousness, just having a place to eat together is important. I have mentioned that the phrase "breaking of bread" in the book of Acts probably refers to the early communion service. If it doesn't, it simply refers to a church supper! And if it does refer to something more formal, it shows—as does Paul's rebuke to the Corinthians (I Cor. 11:20-34) —that our most sacred rite grew out of a church supper! I have been, I suppose, to as many church suppers as the average person, and I have eaten through at least my first mile of meat loaf; I know the hazards of pot luck suppers. I know that a local church ought not to become a knife-and-fork club, nor put on bean suppers every week to "raise money." But I am sure that a place to eat together is essential to creating a growing friendliness in any church.

More than this, a church can increase fellowship through the continual creation of new fellowship groups —small groups of fifteen or twenty people, which are small enough, usually, to meet in members' homes as did the church of the New Testament. Such groups ought not to be only for couples; why not one for single parents and divorcees, who so often are unintentionally cut off from ordinary circles of social intercourse? These

could eventually lead to some kind of full-scale parish
plan which perhaps might do for our day something of
what John Wesley's class meetings did for his. Such
groups are not an incidental part of the church's life;
they are not just social frosting on the religious cake;
they are part of the leaven that permeates and raises
the whole.

There was a book published several years ago with a
striking title. I never read the book, and I haven't the
slightest idea what it was about, but I have never for-
gotten its title: *You Can't Build a Chimney from the
Top*. Surely that is obvious! But why can't you? Because this universe is put together in such a way that the
higher always has to rest on the lower; the organic rests
on the inorganic, and the higher forms of life—clear
up to man at the top of the scale—rest on, and have
been built up from, the lower. The same thing is true
in a scale of values. Surely it is a higher value to read a
book or paint a picture or write a psalm than it is to eat
a meal. But if people don't or can't get food enough, it
isn't very long before there aren't any books read or
pictures painted or psalms sung. The same thing is true
in character. No one ever built it from the top, although there are quite a few who get by for a while on
their personalities, laying bricks out in thin air and
mortaring them together with glib clichés.

The same thing is true of fellowship; it can't be built
from the top any more than a chimney can. No church
staff can create it for the membership; no building, however well planned, will produce it. It is built up from

the bottom a brick at a time. And few things help to build it more than the experiences which come from sacrificially working and giving together. Do not quietly avoid getting involved and let someone else do it! Even if you yourself feel no need for additional fellowship, the fellow next to you may not be so fortunate, and the Good Book tells us to "bear one another's burdens" (Gal. 6:2) and "as we have opportunity" to do good to all (Gal. 6:10), especially our fellow churchmen!

Here is what the fellowship of the church can do:

The counseling you gave us Friday night was most helpful and brought questions to a head between us that had to be answered before we went any further. We had a long talk after we left you and got many things settled. Sometimes this love business throws things so sky-high that not much practical thinking gets done. May we tell you how much you helped us and encourage you to continue to help others likewise.

It was the fellowship of our church, extended through me, that helped to get that young couple off to a good start! Or take note of this letter from a college student who was sending back a filled Lenten sacrificial offering folder:

When I first looked at my folder, I thought, ten cents a day isn't much to ask for or much to give. After thinking of what it would mean to me, I hope it will mean as much in God's work. A dime to a college student means a cup of coffee at ten o'clock so you can face your next lecture; $3.80

means four shows complete with popcorn or a dinner out to relieve the monotony of the institutionalized food we are served. Believe me, this close to the end of the term a few extra dollars seem like a small fortune. . . . Yet if in some small way this money could help someone find the pleasure that comes from knowing God, it will be better spent than on the aforementioned pleasures.

This is an example of the fellowship of the church helping a student in a small but real way.

In the closing months of the Civil War the Federal troops had gained an edge in the fighting in the Shenandoah Valley. General Philip Sheridan was eager to follow up the advantage. In the thick of an attack he came upon a brigade which was winded and had stopped to get its breath; he reined up, gesturing toward the retreating Confederates, and shouted, "Run, boys run! Don't wait to form! Don't let 'em stop!" A soldier shouted back that for the moment they were too bushed to run, to which Sheridan replied, "If you can't run, then holler!" And holler they did, to give spirit to those who were pressing the pursuit.

That is what I ask now. Everyone can have some part in the church's fellowship. "If you can't run, then holler!"

What every human needs is fellowship; hundreds in every community and millions in this world are hungering and thirsting for it. You may be thinking to yourself that, despite these brave words, we really can't do much about it. But we can! Most of the great advances for humanity have been made by small groups moved by great convictions to do great things—Jesus and his twelve; Paul's Churches, so small they met in members' homes; Columbus and three small ships; and the Declaration of Independence signed by a handful; the Wright brothers and Lindbergh; those brave men eulogized by a great leader: "Never in all history have so many owed so much to so few." Let us then enter with joy into the work given us to do and count ourselves fortunate to be part of those called to build a truer and nobler fellowship of kindred minds.

The Measure of a Church

A few years ago an international conference on weights and measures made a wave length of light the new official standard of length. "The meter is now defined as 1,650,763.73 wave lengths of the . . . light given off by electrically excited krypton 86. . . . The U.S. inch is 41,929.399 wave lengths." There may not be very many people to whom that makes very much difference. When I was a schoolboy, I was taught about a platinum bar which was kept at a constant temperature in some basement in Paris. Near the ends of that bar were microscopically thin lines, the distance between which was exactly one meter, the ultimate world standard of measurement. I have always found that close enough for my work and I suppose that you have for yours. Not having any krypton handy myself, I haven't gotten around to checking the wooden yardstick some store gave me free years ago against the new standard; in fact, I hadn't even checked it against the old platinum bar, so my measurements may have been pretty far off all the time.

All lightheartedness aside, we all recognize the need for an ultimate standard of measure, and we can at least dimly comprehend that the infinitesimally small variance of a few units in a million, possible under the old standard, when translated into guidance systems for space exploration could easily cause a space probe to miss its target by thousands or even millions of miles.

Like everything else, a church needs to be checked against a standard, against an ideal, from time to time to see if it is on target and if it measures up to what it should be. A convenient way of going at it is suggested by several lines from the Revelation, one of those exotic visions of John, which are at first glance about as remote from most of us as a wave length of light from krypton 86: "Then I was given a measuring rod like a staff, and I was told: 'Rise and measure the temple of God and the altar and those who worship there'" (11:1-3). This passage suggests a way to measure every church.

I

The first thing John was told to do was to "measure the temple of God." One thing to do in measuring a church is to *assess its building.* We all know that the physical building is not the final consideration nor the most important thing about a church. But let us not forget that the very physical structure has its part to play in the purposes of God. The higher values always rest upon the lower, and just as books are more important than cafeterias to a university, worship and education and fellowship are surely more important to a church than its building. But if a person is denied food very long, he will soon have no need for, or ability to use, books. And worship, education, fellowship, and everything else which is part of true church life depend in part upon physical facilities.

What about the building, then? Does it measure up? Is it adequate? Some of us are extremely fortunate; we can be thankful for the general excellence of a plan and architecture which age will not wither but only mellow. But even that does not necessarily mean that a building is in good operating condition. Sometimes work begun years earlier has never been completed; sometimes the walls are grimy from years of use without repainting. A member once wrote to a minister that she hoped the repainting of the fellowship hall would be included in the building campaign. "It used to be," she wrote wistfully, "a very lovely room." She didn't mention it, but before the room needed repainting it needed ceiling repair where a roof leak had once caused the plaster to fall through! Sometimes a church needs to have its stained glass panels made as good as new. I once saw one which had a hole the size of a lemon in it. And even the best of windows grow loose in their leaded joints and bulge from the contraction of winter's cold and the expansion of summer's heat. Sometimes the exterior paint is cracked and peeling. Sometimes good classrooms cannot be used because the standards of fire safety are higher now than they used to be, and a fire escape is required. There is usually much to be done before we can honestly say that a building is in good condition.

One of the most famous lectures ever given on this continent was called "Acres of Diamonds." It was given more than six thousand times between 1875 and

1900; it is still in print, and you still occasionally run into someone who remembers hearing it in person. Its author was Dr. Russell Conwell, a Philadelphia preacher. In the early days of his ministry he once came into the entryway to his church and found a little girl crying. He gently asked her why she was crying, and she told him that there wasn't any room for her in Sunday school. Their facilities were then, as many are now, inadequate. Dr. Conwell took the child in his arms, wiped away her tears, and promised her that someday they would have a church with room enough for all the children who wanted to come in.

A few months later the little girl tragically died. Her grief-stricken father brought Dr. Conwell the bank in which his little girl had been saving her pennies to build the new church. When they opened it, they found it contained fifty-seven cents. Not much, but Dr. Conwell took the bank into the pulpit one Sunday soon thereafter and told what lay behind that gift. And a great congregation, inspired by her use of what she had, pledged half a million dollars to the building of a new church. Most churches may not need half a million dollars for a building program, but if a church is to render a significant service to its community, it needs an adequate building.

II

The second thing John was told to do was to measure the altar. *Another factor to consider in evaluating a church is its ministry,* the ones who officiate at the altar.

111

For me to say anything in evaluation of ministers would be a little like that celebrated book which was called *An Unbiased Account of the War Between the States from a Southern Point of View!* I can, however, at least try to say something of what I believe a minister's purpose should be: the work of the ministry is to lead the church in continuing the work of Jesus. That means trying to increase the love of God and neighbor through preaching, teaching, helping, evangelizing, counseling. No one of us, I suppose, can really know how well or how poorly we are doing the job, but from time to time a minister gets a glimpse which gives substance to the faith that God uses our weakness to magnify his power.

Not long ago, for example, there was a three-word note on a friendship card: "You have helped." Helped whom? I did not recognize the name. Helped how—by prayer, sermon, scripture lesson, suggestion? I do not know. Helped over or through what obstacle—intellectual, moral, emotional? Only that person and God know. Or another note on a friendship card: "Thank you for the most meaningful Easter and Communion I have ever had. . . . It is so different from home. Here it seems to have a meaning." What is the value of that kind of influence on a student? Or another, from a visitor from a southern city: "It is a very satisfying thing to find a strong church and also to see worshiping here men of several races." How much could that mean in a world whose greatest problem, next to nuclear suicide itself, is a need for increasing racial tolerance, understanding, and harmony?

112

One of the most encouraging letters I have ever received had this paragraph in it: "I would like to take this opportunity to say that since we moved here four years ago and have attended this church . . . we have grown as Christians. We still have far to go toward living the pattern Jesus set for us." Another said, "Just wanted you to know that my husband and I very much appreciated the broadcast of the Communion Service. While he is much better—which we hope will continue—he is just getting out for a few minutes now and then. . . . It was very meaningful to us both and we wanted you to know."

You are fully aware that these unsolicited testimonials are not the only kind of communication a minister receives; you are able to supply, I am sure, from your own experience or observation, the needed grain of salt to keep the perspective true. One of the ancient church fathers has a paragraph which puts the whole thing, perhaps, in a little more objective frame of reference than any of us could give it:

Many priests there are, and few; many in name, and few in works. See, therefore, how ye sit in the official chair, for the chair does not make the priest, but the priest makes the chair: the place does not sanctify the man but the man the place. Not every priest is holy; but every holy person is a priest. He who sits well in the official chair gives honor to the chair; he who sits there ill does injury to it.

In the tumultuous days leading up to the Civil War two young slave sisters had tried to escape from bondage but were captured and taken to New Orleans for sale. The price set on them was one thousand dollars apiece. Through the father, who was a freedman, the news got to Henry Ward Beecher. He immediately called a meeting to raise enough to buy their freedom. Since their labor would not have been worth a third of the asking price, everyone knew what fate was in store for them if they were sold on the slave market. Beecher read, a phrase at a time, a letter from the auctioneers in which the good points of the girls were set forth. It began with their physical qualities: youth, health, beauty; then went on to mental traits: alert, capable; then to their moral qualifications: honest and obedient; and finally, as their supreme attribute, listed them as "prayin' Methodists." Before he was through, Beecher had sold these girls into freedom—he had raised the money to buy them and set them free. Those who were there said it was one of the most thrilling moments of their lives.

Ministers, it is true, are not often engaged in redeeming two Negroes from slavery. But they are engaged in the only enterprise which has a vision of redeeming the whole world from slavery. In the light of that the ministry of any church is always under judgment for its inadequacy.

III

The third thing John was told to do was to measure "those who worship there." The final question in measuring any church is: *Are the people adequate?*

I think that we can say without any fear of contradiction that the people of most churches are adequate in resources. They often enjoy steady employment; studies consistently show that their incomes are above average for the country. Business is good. The average family now has larger earnings than ever before. We are adequate in resources.

Then again, I think it can be safely said that the people of most churches are adequate in determination. Buildings are not built and rebuilt nor new educational facilities added by people short on tenacity. They usually stick to it until the job is done—even if it takes years to pay off an original indebtedness. For the most part, church people have not been short, in the past at least, on determination.

The only real question is are we adequate in consecration? Are we willing to make the sacrifices necessary to bring our buildings up to snuff and to make reasonable provision for maintaining them in that condition? Are we willing to keep faith with tithing as a personal goal for giving and to take a significant step toward it each year? I have the feeling that if we fall short, the cause will basically be that given by a New Hampshire basketball fan after his team absorbed a 115-54 defeat: "Our biggest trouble is that we had a real poor season last year and most of our players returned." We have not been having poor seasons recently in the church, but we have been giving far below the level of our potential.

Paul compared the Christian life to running a race (I Cor. 9:24) or competing in an athletic contest (II Tim. 2:5). It is an apt comparison. One of the things we learn in sports is that records are made to be broken. About twenty-five years ago a distinguished coach of track and field made a chart estimating the absolute ultimate in human performance in the events of that sport. His estimates were by no means conservative; fellow sportsmen believed him far too bold; the performances he looked for were widely regarded as utterly fantastic. But of the eighteen events in which he set performance goals, the athletic world has now surpassed all but three! Some of the qualifying standards for the 1960 Olympics surpass what he thought of as ultimates. "Very few Olympic champions before 1932 could qualify on their winning performances for a place in the 1960 games." Records are made to be broken!

So also in this matter of stewardship. For many of us tithing, the giving of 10 percent of our income, is a goal, a standard of achievement not yet reached. Perhaps our first real step was to make a pledge; then maybe we have moved on to pledging some definite percentage of our incomes—3 percent, 5 percent, 7 percent. Are we breaking our own records? Is the percentage higher this year than last? Others of us, perhaps, have been tithers for years. Have we stopped there? It is easy to get a little smug about our stewardship! In my opinion, tithing was set as a goal before a people living in an economy of scarcity, and it ought to be surpassed by those like ourselves who live in an economy of abundance, an "affluent society."

In recent years many have received pay raises; in such cases giving the same old amount actually means giving a smaller percentage than before. If we ever get the idea that we have "arrived" in our giving (whether we're giving 2 or 6 or 10 or 12 percent of our incomes), we will find before long that we won't even be around for the qualifying races, to say nothing of the main events. Our personal stewardship records are made to be broken.

When we are trying to measure our stewardship, we must remember that *there is something about steward-ship that sets off a chain reaction for good.* We are all plagued at times with the thought that the little we can do, even at our best, doesn't really make much of an impact on the staggering evils of our time. Even a person with a $15,000 income giving 10 or 12 or 15 percent of it can feel as if his offering is only a drop in the bucket.

It takes only an atom or two to start a chain reaction, and God has a way of magnifying the efforts of faithful stewards. Robert Hill was the thirteen-year-old son of a United States Army sergeant stationed in Italy. He read somewhere about Albert Schweitzer's work in Africa and resolved to help by sending a bottle of aspirin. He got word to the Air Force, asking if sometime they could drop his bottle of aspirin on a flight over the jungle. His request caught the imagination of others; a radio station picked it up as a human interest story. Before long young Robert was flown by French and Italian government planes to the Schweitzer hospital with four and a half tons of medical supplies worth $400,000 freely given by thousands of good-hearted people. Even "the grand doctor," who himself is a magnificent symbol of one man's stewardship setting off a chain reaction for good, commented, "I never thought a child could do so much." Call it incentive, call it example, call it a miracle like the one the boy with five loaves and two fish set off if you want to—but there is something about genuine concern expressed through personal stewardship that sets off a chain reaction for good.

The scientists tell us that even a pebble tossed into the ocean affects everyone of the seven seas that girdle the globe. A widow once dropped a few coppers in the offering box, and the results are still being felt wherever the story of Jesus is told (Mark 12:41-44). At the top of Chinook pass in Mt. Rainier National Park there is a memorial bust of Stephen T. Mather, facing toward the majestic snowcapped peak. Mather was a direct lineal descendant of the famous colonial Puritan family, and his sense of stewardship was no less acute than that of his forefathers. He was the first director of the National Park Service, and it was under his leadership that the principles for the coordination, preservation, and use of the national parks were first laid down. Engraved on the monument are these simple words, "There will never come an end to the good that he has done." Those are great words to stand over any man's life! And they are the substance of what is written in records more enduring than bronze about every faithful Christian steward. We may never exercise positions of high importance nor directly influence any dramatic decisions, but if we are faithful with what we have where we are, there will never come an end to the good which we have done.

The New York Mets remind me of a classic remark by Charlie Grimm, who used to manage the Chicago Cubs. The Cubs were having a disastrous year and were in a long losing streak when one of "Jolly Cholly's" scouts phoned excitedly from the hinterlands. "Charlie," he shouted with joy, "I've just seen the greatest pitcher in the country! He pitched a perfect game; twenty-seven strikeouts. No one even hit a foul ball off of him until there were two out in the ninth. I've got him here now. What should I do?" "Sign the guy who got the foul," said Grimm. "We need hitters." That is what the church needs now, financial hitters, if it is to measure up to the opportunity and the responsibility God has set before us.

A Heart with Fingers

The text for this chapter is from the funny papers. At least that is where I got it. It really goes back to the writings of Joel Chandler Harris of "Uncle Remus" fame. It is an aphorism rooted in that Afro-American folklore which has enriched our culture in so many ways: "A helpin' hand is a heart with fingers."

While the exact words do not appear in Proverbs, or any other biblical book, surely the Bible is a witness to their truth. "A helpin' hand is a heart with fingers"— might that not be the conclusion to Jesus' own parable of the man who fell among thieves and who was befriended by a good Samaritan? The theme of the necessary union of personal and practical expression with exalted thought and feeling runs throughout the Bible. There is stern old Amos warning his people that pious religiosity without ethical action leads only to destruction. There is Paul, soaring to the very heights of religious insight and feeling in setting forth our Christian faith in immortality, climaxing with an exclamation that is all "heart"—"Thanks be to God, who gives us the victory through our Lord Jesus Christ" (I Cor. 15:57) —and without even pausing for breath going on to the "fingers"—"Therefore . . . be steadfast, im-

movable, always abounding in the work of the Lord"
(I Cor. 15:58) —and in the next sentence taking up the
matter of contributions! And there is James, reminding
those who were long on talk and short on action that
"faith apart from works is dead" (2:26) —what you do
is the incontrovertible evidence of whether your religion is alive or dead.

One of John Wesley's colleagues was once in financial
difficulties. Wesley sent him a brief letter:

Dear Sammy: Trust in the Lord and do good; so shalt thou
dwell in the land and verily thou shalt be fed. Yours af-
fectionately,

John Wesley

With it he enclosed a five-pound bank note. By way of
reply the other wrote:

Reverend and Dear Sir: I have often been struck with the
beauty of this passage of Scripture quoted in your good
letter, but I must confess that I never saw such useful
expository notes on it before. I am, Reverend and Dear Sir,
your obedient and grateful servant.

S. Bradburn

A helping hand is a heart with fingers!

I

Every year the church asks for many helping hands,
for people who will give practical expression to their

spiritual interests and concerns. Such a request always brings up at least two questions.

The first question is: *For what is help needed?* And the answer is: *For service to people.* That is what all church giving goes for in the long run—service to people.

Someone once thought up a little budget leaflet which I thought was very clever. Perhaps you have seen it. I haven't seen it recently, and I don't know just why it has gone into oblivion. Maybe it lost its appeal after people had seen it once; maybe it was so devastatingly true that it was hardly funny to the average person. Its theme was simple: "The Church Needs No Money." It went on, in words and cartoons, to show that the church doesn't need a minister to preach and pray and call on the sick—only the people need one; the church doesn't need any fuel oil—only the people need heat to keep warm in the winter. And so on. And it proposed a possible alternative; it suggested that rather than giving money the membership take turns preaching the sermons, calling in one another's homes, conducting funeral services, counseling the perplexed, enlisting and training church school teachers, and so on. And on Sunday every member could bring with him a five-gallon can of oil for the furnace! You get the idea. The only thing money is needed for in any church is for service to people.

The church tries to serve people through pastoral care—regular visits by ministers to the limit of their time—in the hospital, in private homes, in campus groups, and in individual counseling and letter writing. The church tries to serve people through evangelism, making Jesus Christ known, loved, and obeyed. For each new follower of Christ there must be provided hours of instruction in the Bible, the history of the church, the meaning of membership, and the local fellowship. The church tries to serve people through an educational program for all ages, literally from the cradle to the grave, and many have weekday cooperative schools and kindergartens. The church near a campus tries to serve those unique people known as college faculty and students by a program designed to demonstrate the relevance of Christianity to academic life by probing questions and challenging answers. Above all, a church tries to serve people through public worship. Worship is the most important thing a Christian does and the only completely unique service the church offers. Whether or not the experience of one person has been typical of many I do not know, but I am sure that what this person wrote describes an important part of what the church is trying to do for many through worship: "You who plan for the church have a special gift for making each of us in the congregation feel 'involved'—like participants—so that we really *experience* something, not just follow along." For what is help needed? For service to people.

The second question is: *From whom is help needed?* And the answer, of course, is *from the members and friends of the church.* Direct, personal, immediate, and continuing help is needed from each member and friend, including those who listen by radio.

We live, to be sure, in an inflationary time when just making ends meet in personal finances is something of an accomplishment. We know what the man meant who muttered to his wife, "If we'd saved our money during the recession maybe we could afford to live through this prosperity"! Many of us could adopt as our own the couplet of British editor Sir John Collings, who wrote, after his magazine went on the financial rocks:

> For me I never cared for fame;
> Solvency was my only aim.

As with Paul's church at Corinth, not many are wealthy according to worldly standards or occupy positions of eminence and power. Yet we are almost without exception in a position to help.

One of the encouraging incidents in *The Ugly American* tells how an American woman noticed that the women of an Asiatic village were all stooped as from old age, although many were not by any means old. The reason, she discovered, was that they used homemade brooms made from short reeds. She found a place where the same reeds grew long enough to make a broom with which a woman could sweep while standing erect, and by her example got the women of the village to use them. Months later they wrote their appreciation to her and proudly told how graceful their women were becoming. So many a person hurts himself by using a wrong tool! And so many of us are bent and stooped spiritually because of short-handled stewardship!

There may be someone who seriously believes that he is not in a position to help. Let him hear this true experience and then decide for himself.

Tom and I always believed in tithing, and we planned to do it when our income was large enough. But our needs always increased with our rising salary. We moved from an apartment into a house and then into a larger house. A second car was necessary. Keeping up with the neighbors was expensive. For our three children there were dancing, music, swimming, and skating lessons. So we felt we could not afford to tithe. Meanwhile we gave from what was left of our budget.

At the height of our status, Tom got a jolting cut in salary. We sold our impressive home and also our extra car. We could not begin to maintain our standard of living. Missionaries came to our church. We wanted to do our part, but we had to look out for ourselves first. One day, feeling sorry for ourselves, we bought gallery (instead of our usual front center seats) to a music festival. Parking our car, we had to walk through a slum area. The barrenness smote me—squalid rooms, ragged clothing, gaunt people. Farther on was a gospel mission whose recent plea for help I tossed into the wastebasket. There was no money left after I wrote a check for the music tickets.

The next Sunday there was a guest preacher from overseas. Opening with "This is the century of the hungry, helpless, and homeless," he told us the facts of life. Before he ended, the needs of others become stark reality to me. My husband shared my feelings. But how could we help when there was nothing left over? We decided then that we had to give before spending the paycheck. We agreed that by tithing we would have money for human needs. We couldn't afford not to tithe. It wasn't easy to take out one tenth first and then make adjustments. Yet we have never regretted it. Now when I ride the bus, I remember the mother in India who carried her sick baby twenty miles to a mission for medical care.

Since we really wanted it, it has not been a hardship. Our whole family—children fifteen, thirteen, and twelve now—have an awareness of human misery and our duty as Christians to help relieve it. We now can give at least some of the necessities to the distressed and miserable people in the backward regions of the world. A salary cut made us tithers.

Help is needed from every member and friend of the church! And more help is needed every year. Why? Because the cost of living goes up for churches just as it does for others. If you add to that growing pains and an increase in church school attendance, you do not find an increase so surprising. I know of no successful business which is spending less this year than it did last. I do not think that there has been in recent memory a President more devoted to the principle of economical administration than Mr. Eisenhower. During his first campaign he talked about cutting the national budget by forty billion dollars. But each year the march of events forced him to submit increasingly larger budgets, until they were peacetime records! So it is not surprising that church budgets have a tendency to go up.

II

One of the best-selling novels of a few years ago was called *Trustee from the Toolroom*. It was a quiet and unassuming yarn about a quiet and unassuming English machinist named Keith Stewart. Keith had quit working in a factory toolroom to be his own boss. In the basement of his house he had a workshop where he designed and built working engineering models to precise scale. Each week he made a trip to London to deliver a write-up, complete with plans, pictures, and step-by-step instructions, on how to build a model of a clock or a steam engine or something else, to a model builder's magazine. He and his Katie had never had any children.

Keith's sister had married well; her husband was not only of the titled nobility but had also risen to the rank of lieutenant commander in His Majesty's Navy before an early enforced retirement. But they were not people to put on airs; they lived on the economical side of their income and had managed to increase the modest fortune he had inherited. They were now leaving England, planning to sail their own small sailing vessel to the Pacific, and they asked two things of Keith.

The first thing his sister and brother-in-law asked of him was to make a small watertight copper box and fit it into the hull of their boat. It was no problem for him, of course, and he was glad to do it. The other thing they asked was that he and Katie take care of their ten-year-old daughter Janice for five or six months.

Despite the ex-navyman's skillful seamanship, however, their twenty-eight-foot yacht was caught in a tropical storm, driven onto a reef, and both of its occupants were killed.

When they were long overdue at their next port of call and when a report had come from an obscure island that a small vessel had been wrecked and the bodies of a man and woman had been found and buried, a lawyer came to Keith to tell him that the wills which his sister and her husband had executed in London before they left appointed him as the sole trustee for their daughter and her inheritance.

The estate, however, proved to be practically worthless. Their securities had been sold before they left and presumably converted into diamonds—apparently in an effort to evade the British regulations on taking money out of the country. But the diamonds were no place to be found; if they had taken them with them on the yacht, they had likely gone to the bottom of the sea in the disaster.

Keith and Katie, whose combined earnings had barely sufficed for their own modest needs, thus found themselves with an extra mouth to feed. Moreover, they could look ahead and see additional expenses for Janice and her education. Still further, the more he thought about it, the more it appalled him that the youngster should not receive what was rightly hers. The possibility that the box he had made and cemented into the ballast of the ship might hold the fortune belonging to the youngster became a virtual certainty in his mind, and he determined to go halfway around the world to inspect the beached and broken craft for himself, although he was woefully short on resources of either cash or experience for such a venture.

Most of the book is concerned with how he got there —by persistence, by the help of friends and of strangers, by good luck—and how he erected a headstone to mark the lonely graves, retrieved the treasure box undetected, and took the diamonds back to England. As the lawyer said when things were being put in final order, the commander had "made a very wise choice of a trustee."

That is not only a good story. It is a parable of life. Keith Stewart was an ordinary person who found himself confronted with a particular responsibility—the care and education of a ten-year-old youngster who was innocently and rightly used to better things in life than he could ever give her; he felt not only all the weight of legal responsibility, but, more than that, all the weight of moral and personal responsibility for doing the right thing for the child—the thing that her mother and father would have wanted. He was a *trustee,* someone entrusted by others with special responsibility. The easy and unthinking thing to have done would have been to keep on in his accustomed routine, to have some representative sell whatever could be salvaged from the vessel for scrap, to yield to his own common sense and shrug his shoulders that it was all too bad but what could he do about it? But he took his trusteeship seriously; he accepted the responsibility which life had thrust upon him, and at the end you know that while outwardly he is the same mild-mannered and unobtrusive model builder you met at the beginning, he is not little or insignificant in any sense; rather, he has proved adequate to the assignment life handed him. Nobody can do more than that.

This is where we come in. Life has handed us all assignments; there are no two alike. Some seem relatively easy, and some seem relatively hard; some seem prominent; some seem obscure. We are not all equally equipped—some of us have five talents, and some have only one or two. But we are all *trustees*—we have all been entrusted with the gift of life itself. As a psalmist put it in Ps. 49:7, who can "give to God the price of his life"? We have all been entrusted with time—three score years and ten, more or less. We have all been entrusted with some abilities, born and bred into us. We have all been given the gifts of civilization: fire, the wheel, the alphabet, mathematics. None of us created any of these, nor can any of us ever pay for them. They were given or left to us, and we are all, in a literal and actual way, trustees. Some of us are trustees from the classroom; some are trustees from the kitchen; some are trustees from the office. But all of us are like Keith Stewart in that we are inheritors of distinct responsibilities. One of the great questions about us all, then, is whether or not we fulfill and live up to the trust placed in us, or whether we turn out to be people suggested by the person who asked for "Nevil Shute's book, *Refugee from a Toolroom*"! Either we recognize and accept our trusteeship or we run away from it, that's all.

III

The word "trustee" does not appear in the Bible, but surely scripture is a witness to the truth of what we are talking about. More than one of Jesus' parables is about underlings entrusted with responsibilities by their superiors. Paul borrows a word from the legal and business world of his time—the very word from which our word "economist" comes and which meant the manager or administrator of an estate—to drive home the sense of responsibility he feels: "It is required of *stewards* that they be found trustworthy" (I Cor. 4:2). Christianity with its characteristic leap of faith takes the whole precious bundle of life and talents and possessions and says that they have been entrusted to us by God.

We are all pretty much like Mr. Micawber, the famous Charles Dickens character. Mr. Micawber was leaving London in debt. He owed Mr. Traddles forty-one pounds ten shillings and eleven pence halfpenny.

"To leave this metropolis," said Mr. Micawber with a flourish, "and my friend, Mr. Thomas Traddles, without acquitting myself of the pecuniary part of this obligation, would weigh upon my mind to an unsupportable extent. I have, therefore, prepared for my friend, Mr. Thomas Traddles, and I now hold in my hand, a document which accomplishes the desired object. I beg to hand to my friend, Mr. Thomas Traddles, my IOU for forty-one, ten, eleven and a half, and I am happy to recover my moral dignity, and to know that I can once more walk erect before my fellow man!"

We are all like Mr. Micawber, I suggest, in that we all pay part of our way through life with IOUs. We are all indebted—indebted to the parents that gave us life, the earth and sun that sustain it, the friends and institutions that make it worthwhile.

One midnight, deep in starlight still
I dreamt that I received this bill: . . .
5,000 breathless dawns all new
5,000 flowers fresh with dew;
5,000 sunsets wrapped in gold;
1,000,000 snowflakes served ice-cold;
100 music-haunted dreams
Of moon-drenched roads and hurrying streams;
Of prophesying winds and trees;
Of silent stars and browsing bees;
One June night in fragrant wood;
One friend I loved and understood.
I wondered when I waked that day
How in the world I ever could pay!

Certainly this is an idea that saturates the Scriptures. From the Old Testament we read the question of the psalmist, "What shall I render unto the Lord for all his benefits?" (Ps. 116:12 KJV.) In the New Testament we read the question of Paul to the Corinthians, "What have you that you did not receive?" (I Cor. 4:7.) "Every good endowment and every perfect gift is from above," declares James (Jas. 1:17). "Forgive us our debts," prays the Master (Matt. 6:12). Oh, the Bible is full of the consciousness that we are all indebted.

The longer we live, the more surely do we become convinced of it by our own experience. During the presidency of the famous Mark Hopkins at Williams College some village buildings were damaged by irresponsible pranksterism. The culprit was found to be the scion of a wealthy family. Called to account before the president, the young man pulled out his wallet and said jauntily, "Well, Doctor, what is the damage?" The stern reply of President Hopkins sobered him up a little, however. "Put up your pocketbook. Tomorrow at prayers you will make public acknowledgment of your offense or you will be expelled." And speaking later of the incident the renowned educator said: "Rich young men come here and take that tone as if they could pay for what they get here. No student can pay for what he gets in Williams College. Can any student pay for the sacrifices of Colonel Williams and our other benefactors, for the heroic sacrifices of half-paid professors who have given their lives that young men might have a liberal education? Every man here is a charity student."

What is true in the educational realm is true in almost every field to which we turn. No one of us can possibly pay for the good things we have received. Some time ago, according to the papers, an unusually sensitive citizen left a codicil to his will which read, in part, as follows:

Although the foregoing enjoins my executor to pay my just debts and to distribute my worldly possessions in the manner I have indicated, I cannot leave this world without grateful acknowledgment of debts which I have never been able fully to repay, to wit:

To my mother: for the pain and sacrifice of bringing me into the world, for comforting me when hurt, for encouraging me when I have faltered, for forgiving me when I have been disobedient, for loving me, always and forever:

To my father: for setting a pattern of faith and integrity, of modesty and sobriety, of self-control and inner calm, of love and affection beyond anything I have ever known in a fellow man;

To my teachers: for their patience and encouragement;

To my employers: for the opportunity for useful work;

To my friends: for knowing my faults but loving me still;

To my wife: for making a house a home and for giving me, without stint, a companionship, an affection and an understanding beyond price and beyond compare;

To the writers of good books: for sharing their thoughts and experiences;

To martyrs: who, on ten thousand battlefields of mind and body gave me religious and political freedom;

To my fellow workers: for making ways easy that could have been hard;

To my children: for their love and faith;

To my God: for imparting to me the knowledge of good and of evil, for his assurance of forgiveness if I am truly penitent, and for his eternal promises.

All of us, I surmise, could add a few to the list. When we stop to think for even a moment, we know that we are all indebted to the past and to the present, to the seen and to the unseen. Freely have we received. We are all trustees, all debtors, all stewards.

My friend Dr. Darrel Berg is my source for an incident with which I want to close this chapter. A couple of generations ago the citizens of Richmond authorized the erection of a statue of General Robert E. Lee. When the likeness of the beloved leader mounted on his favorite horse Traveler arrived, it would have been routine procedure to have horses and wagons move it from the railroad car to its place on Monument Avenue. But someone had an inspired idea—"Let's pull it ourselves!" The idea swept the city like wildfire; the newspapers featured it; a day was set; schools were closed; flags, bunting, confetti were everywhere; the sidewalks along the route were jammed as for a parade. Through the streets passed the great statue on three wagons lashed together and pulled by human hands. All sorts of people had hold of that rope—millionaires, politicians, Confederate veterans, Negroes, "poor whites," school children, society ladies. So the heavy statue was moved into position. When the job was done, someone took out his pocketknife and cut off a little piece of that great rope; that idea spread as if by magic also, and countless others did the same. And for days afterward strong men and little children, rich and poor would pull out a little piece of hemp to show to their friends, and say: "I had hold of the rope. Did you?"

That would be a great thing for a Virginian, to have had hold of such a rope. How much greater is it then for everyone of us to lend a helping hand in the cause of Christ today through voluntary sacrificial giving! "A helpin' hand is a heart with fingers."

The Richest Man in Babylon

A successful businessman once gave me a little booklet
with the intriguing title *The Richest Man in Babylon*.
Even more intriguing than its title was what it promised
—nothing less than a system to arrive at the goal of
financial plenty. Is there anyone who wouldn't think it
worth looking into?

It is the plainly apocryphal story of Arkad, who lived
in Old Babylon. Arkad was famous not only for his
wealth but for his liberality, yet "each year his wealth
increased more rapidly than he spent it." It had not always been so. He had been born in ordinary circumstances—the son of a merchant, one of a large family;
he had not simply inherited his great wealth. Nor was
he endowed with any particular mental or physical su-
periority which had relatively quickly and easily earned
him a fortune beyond that of his fellows. He hadn't
struck it rich in Klondike gold or Arabian oil. He had
made a normal quota of mistakes and had been the victim
of his own poor judgment a time or two. And yet the time
came when those who had grown up with him but had
remained in less affluent positions all their lives came to
him to ask his secret. They had once been equals; they
had gone to the same school; they had played the same
games; they had been equally honorable citizens and

had worked as hard and as faithfully as Arkad. Yet he was wealthy and they were little more than making ends meet. How had he done it?

He told them that the solid foundation of his fortune was laid when he learned from a rich man that a part of all he earned was his to keep. It sounded so simple and so obvious that he had had trouble believing it. Wasn't *all* he earned his to keep? No, it wasn't, the other had pointed out. He had to pay to butcher, the baker, and the candlestick maker. He couldn't live in Babylon without spending money. He was spending all he was earning. He never had anything to show for a year's work. His mentor went on: "A part of all you earn is yours to keep. It should not be less than a tenth no matter how little you earn. . . . Pay yourself first. Do not buy . . . more than you can pay out of the rest." And according to the story Arkad began to save, then to invest his savings; his wisdom and prudence caught the eye of his mentor, and he was invited to manage his estates and eventually became his partner, successor, and "the richest man in Babylon."

I suppose you might call it a sort of Arabian Nights Horatio Alger story. It leaves a good deal to be desired from the standpoint of economic theory. Yet the moral of the tale—the value of thrift, of living on less than you earn—is surely a sound one and is ignored by anyone at his own peril. "A part of all you earn is yours to keep."

Important as that is, however, there is a similar but deeper and better principle according to the Bible. There is something greater even than being the richest man in Babylon, and it is toward that that I turn your attention now. What is it? *A part of all you earn is yours to give.* It is better to be a cheerful giver than to be the richest man in Babylon because to save but not give guarantees only that one will finally be the richest man in the cemetery. We are thinking then, about Christian giving. We are thinking about it not in connection with any specific financial campaign; we are thinking about it not as a means of erasing deficits or meeting church budgets. We are thinking about giving as one of the core ingredients in the life of a Christian. And there are three or four things to say about it.

I

Giving is the response of the indebted heart. We do not handle our money as real Christian stewards, I am persuaded, until we do so with an overwhelming sense of indebtedness, from a conviction that we have received richly from life and in simple honor can do nothing less than to give generously to life.

People can and do give, of course, from a sense of duty; we are sometimes shamed into giving to some cause or other. And it is undoubtedly better to give that way than not to give at all. Sometimes we give from our desire to be a part of something in which we believe; we want to maintain and extend its influence. And there is something to be said for that kind of motivation. Some people give as a means of spiritual discipline, an exercise to strengthen their moral character. And if the gift is large enough and regular enough to involve doing without something they'd really like to have or do, it will certainly help to develop moral physique, so to speak. It is a great thing to be able to deny as well as to indulge ourselves. But people do not really reach the heights of Christian giving until they have matured beyond these levels. We never really are convinced that a part of all we earn is ours to give until we are overwhelmed with our own indebtedness.

A few years ago one of the most sensitive of our American journalists visited Albert Schweitzer's mission hospital in Africa. He couldn't help asking the staff members why they were there, why they had given up so much to work for subsistence pay in an obscure corner of the Dark Continent. A young German doctor, who had lost all his relatives in concentration camps during and following the war, gave the clearest answer:

Some of us have come here because we were in good circumstances and didn't feel quite right about it [as Schweitzer himself had]; others because they were in difficult circumstances yet managed somehow to survive [as he himself had], and they wanted to find some way of acknowledging their debt. But always it is the debt. And always you will find that somewhere he happened to read something about Albert Schweitzer that opened a big door in our mind and made us know we had to come.

Always it is the debt. And always you will find that somewhere something opened a big door in our minds and made us come. This is the key that always unlocks the secret of Christian stewardship whether of time, of talents, or of money. It unlocks the kind of giving that makes one richer than the richest man in Babylon. "I am debtor," says Paul, "both to the Greeks, and to the Barbarians" (Rom. 1:14 KJV). Giving is the response of the indebted heart.

II

The second thing to say about the exciting discovery that part of all we earn is ours to give is just what Arkad learned about saving: *"It should not be less than a tenth."* Tithing—the regular, systematic giving of 10 percent or more of one's income—is one of the best ways religious men have ever found of giving practical expression to the indebtedness they feel to life. It has withstood well the test of time. It was effective in that far-off time of which we read in Gen. 28:10-22. Jacob had had a wonderful dream in natural color about a ladder to heaven. In contemporary terms he had had a psychic experience of some sort; in biblical terms it was an experience of God. But whatever you call it and however you define it, it moved him to vow that of all life gave him he would give a tenth. It is effective now. A man in a church I once served puts his own experience in somewhat less classical phrases than those of Genesis, but perhaps for that very reason you will understand even better what he means:

I heard a minister suggest a six months' trial of tithing as a means of approach to a better spiritual understanding. Well, I had tried about everything so my wife and I decided to try it. We seemed seldom to have enough money to pay current bills anyway. We took 10 percent off the top and divided the rest between food, clothing, taxes, etc. Do you know what happened? The old paycheck seemed to develop a two-way stretch just like a modern girdle. It covered the whole situation and firmed up our spiritual foundations. After six months we had a full head of steam and couldn't stop. We didn't want to. . . . We didn't even bother looking back. . . . We have had rich experiences of God. We want more of them. Tithing is the way.

Do not get me wrong. I am not among those who say that if you'll only start tithing all your troubles will disappear, the bottom of your financial well will never go dry but increase almost miraculously. Tithing—at least for people in the ordinary circumstances of life— means self-discipline and self-denial. I once heard a good Christian exclaim: "I used to think you could tithe and have everything else too. But now I know you can't. You have to give up something." What he and his family were giving up was a nice home- moving to more modest housing, in order to keep on tithing! If you don't have to cut your standard of living—your food budget, your clothing budget, your family recreation— in order to raise your standard of giving to the minimum biblical level of 10 percent, then you should be giving more than 10 percent.

III

The third thing to say is that *nothing less is going to do the job*. American Christianity by the providence of

God is in a position to play a crucial role in human affairs. We have profited from a political system which gives Christianity the most favorable circumstances of any in which to work. We have profited from an industrial revolution made to order for a continent of vast unused resources. We have profited from a remarkable succession of leaders in political thought, mechanical ingenuity, technological creativity, social insight, and religious dedication. We have profited from a sort of natural selection of hardy, venturesome, ambitious immigrants. And we stand in a position to influence the destiny of the world. American Christians by the providence of God have been given an opportunity to speak and act at a critical and strategic moment in history.

But by comfortably feathering our own nests we are not going to influence for good a world threatening to commit suicide, nor by ignoring the bulk of humanity or admonishing them to be as patient and industrious and thrifty as we. We are already the richest man in Babylon; unless we can do better than that, our wealth and security and freedom are literally going to turn to radioactive dust and ashes. I do not know whether learning that at least 10 percent of all we earn is ours to give will do the job through the medical, agricultural, and educational missionary-ambassadors of Christian good will it would make possible. But I am as sure as I can be that nothing less than that will suffice. As far as our civilization is concerned, we are now playing for keeps. "A Communist," according to a considerable authority on the subject, Nikita Khrushchev, "has no right to be a mere onlooker." Must it be that once again the children of darkness will prove wiser in their own generation than the children of light? I do not know what it will take to get the world through its current time of troubles in any kind of inhabitable shape, but it is pretty clear that anything less than voluntary giving of 10 percent and more by American Christians will be too little and too late.

IV

The fourth thing to say about the principle that not less than 10 percent of all we earn is ours to give is that *tithing can be a means of grace.* It can be the channel through which God does something fine to people. It can be a highway to broader interests, enlarged concerns, deeper involvement, and greater satisfactions.

During World War II our natural sources of quinine were cut off at the very time we were needing more than ever to protect our servicemen in malaria infested areas. A team of medical researchers asked the inmates of the Atlanta Penitentiary for volunteer human guinea pigs in the attempt to discover a suitable substitute. About three hundred men responded, were infected, and provided the living laboratories that made possible the development of chloroquinine. When the work was completed, every man was given an emblem to wear on his sleeve, but one refused it, saying, "I don't want any credit—this was the only decent thing I ever did." He was neither the first nor the last to learn that the voluntary giving of one's self brings an inner satisfaction that is beyond any outward recognition.

I have said that tithing *can* be a means whereby God does something fine to people. I am well aware that there are tithers who are legalistic, hard-shelled, dried-up, juiceless, and nearly useless as far as the kingdom is concerned. Such people often drive others away from Christianity rather than drawing them winsomely toward it. But surely it is not fair to judge tithing by its worst representatives! When I think back over those I have known personally, I can think of one or two who were that way. But I can also think of a great many who were the warmest, friendliest, most consecrated people I have ever known, people who were a lift to anyone's spirit, people who were always on the leading edge of worthwhile community projects. To a man they all agreed that tithing had helped to make them what they were. It can be a means of grace.

Tithing is not an end in itself. It is a practice which leads us toward two other biblical attitudes with respect to money. One of these is the *attitude of liberality.* The Bible says that we should contribute "in liberality" (Rom. 12:8). Liberal giving is the opposite of miserly giving, of stinginess. It is something more than carefully calculating one's "share" of any worthy cause, too. It has the feel—as it should have, being related to liberty —of "free and easy" about it. The liberal gift is the one which is more than anyone would have had a right to

144

expect you to give. It is giving as Paul put it to the Corinthians, with "great generosity" (II Cor. 9:11).

Sometimes we almost seem to take the attitude that we ought not to give, nor the church expect, liberal gifts. I suppose it's a hangover from the Puritan reaction against luxuries and adornments in religion or anywhere else. It may also be at least partly an inheritance from the rugged simplicity demanded of and exercised by the pioneers who won the West. A description of pioneer church furnishings in what was the West a hundred years ago was written by a visitor in a letter to a friend in the more cultured and affluent East in these words: "The seats were free—free from upholstery, free from paint, free from backs. . . . They were the poorest kind of seats in which to take a nap during the sermon." I am willing to admit that the Puritan reaction may have been necessary to drag Christianity back from the sensuous opulence of the Renaissance and the unholy alliance of wealth and political power in medieval Christianity. And I certainly have no quarrel with frontier frugality and simplicity. But the Bible does not take the attitude that our religious institutions should be spartan and unadorned, or our place of worship severe in its austerity.

On the contrary, the biblical point of view is that we should give of our very best for God and that the house of God should be treated royally. The Israelites were expected to bring the first and finest fruits of their industry as their offering. In Exodus we read that the Lord said to Moses, "Speak to the people of Israel, that they take for me an offering; from every man whose heart makes him willing you shall receive the offering for me. And this is the offering which you shall receive from them: gold, silver, and bronze, blue and purple and scarlet stuff and fine twined linen, goats' hair, tanned rams' skins, goatskins, acacia wood, oil for the lamps, spices for the anointing oil and for the fragrant incense, onyx stones, and stones for setting. . . . And let them make me a sanctuary, that I may dwell in their midst. (25:1-8.)

That may not sound particularly exciting to you, but the archaeologist and historian tell us that every item on the list was a costly and luxurious one in the ancient world. When they came to build their first temple, we read that it was seven years in the building, and covered —inside and out—with an overlay of pure gold (I Kings 6:21-22, 38) . When it needed repair, they collected money "in abundance" to do the job (II Chron. 24: 11) .

The other biblical word about stewardship which tithing helps us to fulfill is *faithfulness.* "It is required in stewards," says Paul, "that a man be found faithful (I Cor. 4:2 KJV) . One of the recurring words in Jesus' story about the talents is the word *faithful:* "Well done, good and faithful servant; you have been faithful over a little, I will set you over much" (Matt. 25:21) . "Who then," asked our Lord rhetorically on another occasion, "is the faithful and wise steward?" (Luke 12:42.) As far as the Bible is concerned, we ought to be faithful in our giving.

There is a lot of giving which is something less than faithful. In the days before the late President Kennedy nominated Arthur Goldberg for Associate Justice of the Supreme Court, he had a story he told about Goldberg. According to the account Goldberg had gone mountain climbing to get away from it all for awhile. He was gone so long that his friends became alarmed, and the Red Cross was asked to help search for him. They sent a helicopter over the area where he had last been seen with a powerful loudspeaker blasting out at frequent intervals, "Arthur Goldberg, this is the Red Cross." There was no answer at first, but finally a faint voice from the wilderness below replied: "This is Goldberg. I gave through the office this year." That has both a smile and a truth in it, for much of our giving is only in response to dragnet type campaigns which almost have to shame us into contributing, or at least which dare not miss anyone because it has become axiomatic that no one takes the initiative to give voluntarily.

The Bible expects a Christian steward to be faithful —to be trustworthy, responsible, alert to need, ready to take some initiative, ready to give regularly from some inner sense of loyalty and devotion rather than only as a response to outward pleas or pressures.

A few years ago Adlai Stevenson, who was then a private citizen, traveled in Africa to learn firsthand something of the problems and possibilities of that great continent. One of the things that impressed him was the work that Christian missionaries had done there, and upon his return he wrote his testimony:

Anyone who travels there is constantly reminded of their [the missionaries'] heroism. Missionaries laid a groundwork in religion, health, and education under difficult and dangerous circumstances. What they have done is almost beyond belief. They fought yellow fever, dysentery, parasites. And the gravestones I saw! My God, their gravestones—all through Africa.

That is faithfulness unto death, a faithfulness which, by the providence of God, few of us will ever be called upon to exhibit. But how small a thing such faithfulness makes mere faithfulness in giving our money look! The Bible clearly expects us to be faithful in our stewardship.

There is a tradition in the Marines about an officer speaking to a platoon. There was need, he said, for three men for a dangerous mission. He knew that he could simply order three to go and they would go. But he had decided instead to ask for volunteers. "I am going to turn my back," he said, "and give three men the opportunity to move forward one step." He waited a moment or two, then faced the ranks once more. A look of irritation crept over his face; he didn't see three men out of rank, nor two, nor even one. Then the sergeant spoke up, "Sir, the entire platoon has stepped forward." So it is in the Christian life. No one is requiring us to give a tenth of what we earn; it is entirely voluntary. But what a great thing it is when every man in the platoon takes that one step forward!

The Meanest Mortal Known

That man who lives for self alone
Lives for the meanest mortal known.

And when he saw him he passed by on the other side.
(Luke 10:31.)

This is one of the simplest and noblest among the fine
gallery of stories in the Gospels. You remember how
it begins, "A man was going down from Jerusalem to
Jericho, and he fell among robbers, who stripped him
and beat him, and departed, leaving him half-dead."
The name of the man is not given. No hint as to his na-
tionality or race or color or religion or politics or class
or morality is to be found. Whether he was prudent or
foolish does not enter into the discussion. We know a
little more about the other three main figures; the
priest and the Levite were clearly devout religious men.
They were men of substance and position in the civic
life of Jerusalem. They were direct descendants of the
founding fathers of the land, "Sons of the Hebrew
Revolution" so to speak. They had taxes to pay and affairs to manage. And they were too busy or too clean or
too something to stop and get mixed-up in a messy situation; they passed by on the other side. "But a Samaritan,

as he journeyed, came to where he was." This man wasn't kosher; his religion was unorthodox; his politics were subversive; he was a half-breed—a product of the amalgamation and mongrelization of separate races through interracial marriages. He was some distance down on the ladders of respectability and success. It is not likely that he had as regular an income as the others; there is no reason to think that he had more time on his hands than they did. He doesn't appear to have been interested in making a convert of this man to his own way of political or religious thinking. All that he had that the others lacked was compassion. He had, in J. B. Phillips' phrase, "practical sympathy." He had the idea that anyone who needed help that he was in a position to give was his neighbor. Whatever else might be said, you can't say this of him:

> That man who lives for self alone
> Lives for the meanest mortal known.

And when he saw him he passed by on the other side.

I

Tom Dooley is dead. Not the Tom Dooley of the sometime popular hit tune, but the Dr. Thomas Dooley who brought modern medicine to the hinterlands of Laos and whose death by cancer was mourned by so many and added its own minor chord to what he himself called "the sad song of humanity in our time."

The Burma Surgeon, Dr. Seagraves, is dead. His work

was the subject of a moving television documentary. The people who came in a steady stream to his clinic were wonderful to see—some as frail as an El Greco saint; some with delicate, creamy skin and eyes so dark that to look into them was to look into a bottomless pool; some twisted and bent and broken; some little children with the spindly legs and potbellies of malnutrition; some babies so sick that they couldn't even cry.

Albert Schweitzer is dead; he labored in Africa for fifty years. He gave up two established careers—one as a New Testament scholar and the other as one of the world's foremost authorities on Johann Sebastian Bach —in order to treat primitive savages for hernia and dysentery and leprosy.

The late Prime Minister Verwoerd led the nation of South Africa out of the British Commonwealth rather than accept the idea of racial equality. Many a white South African deplores those policies and the increasing ascendancy they have been gaining in recent years. At least one white South African is uncomfortably aware that he didn't do much to oppose such policies and was more than ready to accept the personal comforts and privileges they bestowed upon him. He sent a letter to the Johannesburg *Star* that "was part taunt and part self-mockery":

After two days of soul searching, I have decided to back Dr. Verwoerd and the Nationalist government. I shall do so for the same reason that cinema audiences cheered the Prime

Minister when he appeared on newsreels, for the same reason that kept hundreds of English-speaking South Africans from raising a public outcry. . . . I want to preserve the easy life. I want to preserve my top-dog status in a land where cheap labor is really cheap. I want to ensure that for the rest of my life . . . I shall always have somebody about to do the menial jobs . . . like digging holes, . . . looking after the younger children, fetching and carrying, serving . . . my guests and waiting at my table. I want to be sure too that my sons will have no serious competition in their careers, and that the jobs they eventually choose will be the soft jobs with "master" status. To hell with the rest of the world. I want to be boss.

I leave it to you. Does Tom Dooley, a Burma Surgeon, a massive Schweitzer, or one who wants to be boss above all else come closer to reproducing the spirit of Jesus' story?

> That man who lives for self alone.
> Lives for the meanest mortal known.

And when he saw him he passed by on the other side.

II

I do not mean to be overly subtle; I want to be just as clear and plain as I can in regard to missions—*Christian missions.* I want to enlist your practical sympathy. I want to start you thinking about what you personally are doing for others. I want to start you thinking in terms of making a pledge to missions or, if you are already pledging, of increasing your giving for others. There are some who, for one reason or another, have reservations about missions. Some may think it odd to talk about giving more for others when we are far from being out of the woods as far as local expenses are concerned. Some may have a sneaking suspicion that missionary enterprises are still geared primarily to proselyting, to converting people from their own religion to Christianity. You may have the feeling that you are already giving about as much as you can give. I am sympathetic to all these feelings; at one time or another I have harbored them all myself. But they no longer carry much weight with me personally for just two reasons: Jesus' story with its inescapable point that whoever needs me is my neighbor and a growing conviction that the essence of the contemporary mission enterprise is "helping people to help themselves." That isn't my phrase. It is quoted from the annual report of one of the most remarkable outgrowths of home missions, the Goodwill Industries.

The Goodwill Industries began in the mind of a preacher in an inner city church. He knew people who were throwing things away. He knew people who needed jobs. He knew people who couldn't afford to buy new things. He arranged to have people save the throwaways. He put the unemployed to work on collecting, sorting, repairing, and selling them. He invited those who couldn't afford new things to buy them. He used the money from sales to meet the payroll. And everyone was helped. He was also a great slogan maker; some of them sound a little sticky now: "Never too weak to win," "Never too poor to pray." That was half a century ago.

Today Goodwill pays out millions of dollars a year in wages. One of its earliest slogans might well stand for our entire mission outreach—"Not charity, but a chance." "Charity," noble in origins, has come to have a poor meaning to many; it signifies handouts, a dole, paternalism. That is exactly what the man who had fallen among robbers needed in order to be able to help himself. But it more often now means programs of medical clinics, preventive sanitation, education, nutritional improvement, worship, vocational training, leadership development. It is a human program; it has its faults; it makes its mistakes; it is doubtless not handled in every respect just as you or I would handle it. But at least it saves us from this:

That man who lives for self alone.
Lives for the meanest mortal known.

And when he saw him he passed by on the other side.

III

There is at least one hardheaded, no-nonsense, businesslike reason for missions: they are an intensely practical application of the truth that *the best defense is a good offense.* Christianity has been under fire many times throughout the centuries. It was born and baptized, so to speak, under persecution. And it early learned and has ever remembered that its best defense lies in a good offense. The dark ages of the church are notable for their lack of missionaries; the church, being accepted, became complacent and then stagnant. Feeling no need of defense, it lost its offense. But when it has been under fire—at Jerusalem, in the Roman catacombs, when the Reformation broke out, during the "enlightenment" of the eighteenth century,—then it has been aggressively missionary as its own best means of self-preservation.

General Maurice, in analyzing the men and campaigns of the Civil War, draws this distinction between Robert E. Lee and his predecessor as commander of the Army of Northern Virginia, J. E. Johnston. When the Federal forces, early in the war, were hammering at the approaches to Richmond, the Confederate capital, General Johnston saw no alternative to massing the largest number of troops around Richmond and there hazarding battle. But Lee saw that the best way to relieve the pressure on his own capital city was to threaten that of the North—Washington—and so make the Northern armies return home to defend their own. Lee saw that his best possible defense was in a good offense.

The same thing is true in business. Some time ago a research organization investigated the methods businessmen used to increase sales. They reported that the highest number, 41 percent of the total, said that they add more salesmen. When conditions put a company on the defensive, smart management tries to put it on the offensive.

It isn't any secret that Christianity is under fire today. Secularism and communism are openly out to get us. The *Playboy* philosophy is a glossy version of hedonism which has always scoffed at Christian values. Historians are talking about the "post-Christian" era. If we are to survive at all, it may well be because we discovered anew the old truth that the best defense is a good offense.

Then again, the mission movement of the church is *a sign of life*. Perhaps the surest sign of life available is growth. If the plants in your garden put forth leaves, you know they are alive. If they don't, you know they're dead. Life means growth. In the human realm even adults—who are supposed to have achieved their maximum physically (although someone has defined an adult as "a person who has quit growing at the ends and begun to grow in the middle") —have to show signs of moral, intellectual, and spiritual growth or they are to all intents and purposes dead. As Bishop Kennedy wrote not long ago, "When our religious experience seems quite adequate and we are no longer interested in more light and greater spiritual power, it is time to dig the grave and have a brief, sad service over our spiritual corpse. When men stop growing, men are dying."

So also with the church. When its missionary giving stops growing, it is dying. The normal pattern of Christian experience seems to go something like this: help us, teach us, use us. At least that is the way it went in Paul's first church in Europe, that at Philippi. You will recall that Paul had a dream in Troas, a dream in which he saw a European saying, "Come over . . . and help us"

(Acts 16:9). Paul went; he established a church at Philippi. It grew in knowledge and in grace under the teaching of Paul and his successors until that day when Paul needed some help in another place, and these people then sent financial assistance (Phil. 4:15). They were the first ones of whom there is any record that they contributed to the propagation of Christianity beyond their own city limits. And so it has gone: "It was a Jew who brought the gospel to Rome, a Roman who took it to France, a Frenchman who took it to Scandinavia, a Scandinavian who took it to Scotland, a Scotsman who evangelized Ireland, and an Irishman who in turn made the missionary conquest of Scotland. No country ever originally received the gospel except at the hands of an alien." Growth is a sign of life!

> That man who lives for self alone,
> Lives for the meanest mortal known.

And when he saw him he passed by on the other side.

IV

It may be that the biggest reason that more of us do not get very excited over missions is not so much that we don't "believe" in them as that *our imaginations have never been fired by personal experience.* As Harry Golden puts it, "The great sadness of our history is that the mortal imagination cannot summon the same grief for the casualties of an earthquake that it can for one little girl" who has been hit by a car on our block. If, on your way home from church today, you were to see a man drag another off at gunpoint, then mistreat, torture, and finally kill him, your horror and indignation would know few limits. But it is hard for us even to imagine that an Adolf Eichmann could have planned and ordered it done to 6,000,000 people. We have not seen and cannot imagine the conditions under which most people of Asia, Africa, and South America live, and it is easy not to get very worked up about them.

In the epilogue of George Bernard Shaw's play *St. Joan,* the chaplain says that he knows now that he has been saved. "Saved," unctiously remarks the bishop, "by the sufferings of Christ." "No," says the chaplain, "saved by seeing a young woman actually burned to death. One had to see it to feel the horror of it." And then the bishop puts a searching question, "Must then a Christ perish in torment in every age to save those who have no imagination?" That, as I see it, is the only validity in the trial of Adolf Eichmann—perhaps it dramatized before the world the ghastly devilishness of which even educated and civilized people are capable when corrupted by absolute power. Dramatized it that we may be more cautious about selling our birthrights of freedom and civil liberties for a mess of communist pottage on the left or John Birch societies on the right. Or must true loyalty and genuine patriotism be crucified afresh to save those who have no imagination? Must there be a decline and fall of Western civilization because we have no imagination? Must millions of Asiatics and Africans pull themselves up from poverty and ignorance and ill health, and in the process go to extremes of bitterness and violence, because in our prosperous affluence we have no imagination and no practical sympathy?

I for one do not believe it. I believe that it is not yet too late; I believe that programs under the United Nations, VISTA, and the Peace Corps hold almost measureless hope for humanity. Above all, I believe that the average one of us can do more for others through the voluntary programs of Christian missions than in any other one way—to help people help themselves, to give them not charity but a chance.

> That man who lives for self alone
> Lives for the meanest mortal known.

And when he saw him he passed by on the other side.

V

There is one more thing to say about giving for others: *it brings a bonus of joy and satisfaction that comes in no other way.* There are no words in scripture with more literal truth to them than the line, "It is more blessed to give than to receive" (Acts 20:35). William Allen White, the late great Republican newspaper editor of Emporia, Kansas, gave his town a fifty-acre wooded tract for a park and agreed to beautify and maintain it personally for five years. He was asked why he did it and explained it this way: "I have always felt that there are three kicks in every dollar: one when you make it—and how I do love to make a dollar; one when you have it—and I have the Yankee lust for saving; and the third when you give it away. The last kick is the biggest one of all."

The whole nation shuddered when two giant airliners collided over New York some time ago. Everyone aboard was killed outright except one youngster who lived a day or so. By a strange string of circumstances he had been thrown clear, landed in a snowbank deep enough to cushion his fall, and was found almost immediately and rushed to a hospital. He was badly burned and never had much of a chance of surviving, but as he was lying in the emergency room, he opened his eyes and looked into the face of an attending nurse. She was a stranger, of course, but in his youthful simplicity and trust he said, "I go to Sunday school." And she, trying desperately not to show her own emotions, said, "Then you have come to the right place, because this is a Christian hospital." I do not know what that did to you when you read it. But, in William Allen White's phrase, it gave me one of the greatest kicks of my life to know that you and I and every Christian everywhere have a part in an enterprise which tries always, and succeeds far more often than we know, to be at the right place at the right time to help others!

> That man who lives for self alone
> Lives for the meanest mortal known.

But a Samaritan, as he journeyed, came to where he was; and when he saw him, he had compassion.

160